# DESIGN SCHOOL READER

# DESIGN SCHOOL READER

## A COURSE COMPANION FOR STUDENTS OF GRAPHIC DESIGN

**STEVEN HELLER**

SVA NYC

ALLWORTH PRESS
NEW YORK

Allworth Press books may be purchased in bulk at special discounts for sales
promotion, corporate gifts, fund-raising, or educational purposes. Special
editions can also be created to specifications. For details, contact the Special Sales
Department, Allworth Press, 307 West 36th Street, 11th Floor, New York, NY 10018
or info@skyhorsepublishing.com.

24 23 22 21 20      5 4 3 2 1

Published by Allworth Press, an imprint of Skyhorse Publishing, Inc.

307 West 36th Street, 11th Floor, New York, NY 10018. Allworth Press® is a
registered trademark of Skyhorse Publishing, Inc.®, a Delaware corporation.

www.allworth.com

Copublished with the School of Visual Arts

Cover and interior design by Rick Landers

Library of Congress Cataloging-in-Publication Data

Names: Heller, Steven. Essays. Selections.

Title: Design school reader : a course companion for students of graphic
    design / Steven Heller.

Description: New York, New York : Allworth Press, [2020] | Includes index.

Identifiers: LCCN 2019059993 (print) | LCCN 2019059994 (ebook) | ISBN
    9781621536901 (print) | ISBN 9781621536918 (ebook)

Subjects: LCSH: Graphic arts. | Design.

Classification: LCC NC997 .D4485 2020  (print) | LCC NC997  (ebook) | DDC
    740--dc23

LC record available at https://lccn.loc.gov/2019059993

LC ebook record available at https://lccn.loc.gov/2019059994

Print ISBN: 978-1-62153-690-1

eBook ISBN: 978-1-62153-691-8

Printed in China

Dedicated to Martin Fox, for his editorial guidance
during my years at *Print* magazine.

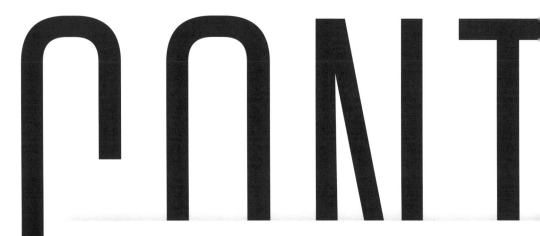

## FOREWORD

## ONE: DESIGN LANGUAGE

## TWO: DESIGN DIALECTS

ENTS

This book is a collection of my essays that I hand out in my Design Reading classes. Well, most are my own, but occasionally they are commentaries or reviews of others' writings. The first of the recommended readings at the beginning of each semester is the artist and illustrator Ben Shahn's "Biography of a Painting" from his book of Harvard lectures, *The Shape of Content*. It seems appropriate to start off this anthology with the story that has inspired me as an art director, writer, and lecturer. It begins with a brief recommendation to readers that I published on DesignObserver.com. It will commence right after the introduction.

# Introduction

*Design School Reader* is how I describe a course, applicable to undergrad and graduate design students, that focuses on reading and writing. Reading is as important as designing—a designer cannot design for readers if they do not also read. In this case, I am proposing that among the great books, articles, and essays related and unrelated to design, students might also dip into some of my own work.

I want to share my musings about graphic design and, more generally, visual communications and popular culture. Building on the premise that all things natural and man-made are designed in the broadest sense, whether intentionally or not, not every essay found here is about conventional design. Yet I hope each text selected will provoke classroom discussion that has some relationship to the practice or history or philosophy of design. There are a range of subjects, many of which have been addressed in my previous anthologies, so I apologize for any duplication. I know my Allworth anthologies, including *Design Literacy: Understanding Graphic Design 3rd Edition* (2014), *The Graphic Design Reader* (2002), *POP: How Graphic Design Shapes Popular Culture* (2010), and *Graphic Design Rants and Raves* (2016), are used as class texts, but this is a little different. *Design School Reader* is specifically formatted as a sum of thematic parts that should be used as content for a class or workshop devoted to reading—not overtly about design, but viewed through the lens of design. Although these are my ideas, this class format (which admittedly is somewhat like a book club) can be done with any bibliography. They key is to read, discuss, and debate; toward this aim, I've included some discussion points at the end of most essays. Over the past couple of decades (before Skype), I would give classes where the students were each required to formulate a few questions based on their reading. I would then answer and we would all discuss. I encourage that participation—and videoconferencing has made it easier.

The selected essays are triggers for discussion. A short precis at the beginning of each section introduces the topic, and at the end I've suggested directions, but they are only suggestions—any and all questions and comments are welcome.

Ultimately, reading should be habitual—it is the gateway to writing—and it is my hope that every design course or program encourages this kind of addiction.

E READ.
RITE READ:

# MY FAVORITE READ: BEN SHAHN'S THE SHAPE OF CONTENT

If you are going to read one thing this year, I suggest
an essay in Ben Shahn's *The Shape of Content* titled
"Biography of a Painting." It is not just about painting
but rather about what is involved in making an image—
a heartfelt image. Since designers are image-makers
and storytellers, the ideas that Shahn, who was a poster
artist, printmaker, book illustrator, photographer, and
painter from the 1920s through the 1960s, addresses
regarding the symbolic composition of his painting
entitled "Allegory" is not only relevant to the muse-
driven elite but to all "applied" or commercial artists
and designers.

*The Shape of Content* is an anthology of lectures given at Harvard in 1957. They address all matters pertaining to Shahn's creation of art. Yet "Biography" explains how art is not immune to the issues of the day, or the news of the moment, but rather is a tool of communicating information and critiquing the world. It is about a painting Shahn made in 1948 that was directly inspired by a news article about a Chicago fire in which "a colored man had lost four children." Shahn was asked to make drawings to accompany a "concise reportorial account of the event." The item was written with the dispassion that was common with such reportage, but after Shahn had acquired all the facts and viewed the visual record of the fire, he decided on a different course.

"It seemed to me," he wrote, "that the implications of this event transcended the immediate story; there was a universality about man's dread of fire, and his suffering of fire." He further noted that it suggested that racial injustice played a role in this event that "had its own kind of universality."

Shahn accounts for why, instead of literally portraying the event, he decided to develop a symbolic framework. "The narrative of the fire," he wrote, "had aroused in me a chain of personal memories." There were two significant fires in his own life, one when he was a boy and the town where he lived had burned down. The other "left its mark upon me and all my family, and left its scars on my father's hands and face, for he had clambered up a drainpipe and taken each of my brothers and sisters and me out of the house one by one, burning himself painfully in the process." As I read this passage, I recalled being pulled out of the fifth floor of my burning apartment building, which killed my next-door neighbor.

The artist describes in vivid terms how he developed symbolic imagery to express the feelings the news and memories evoked—and his search to find the right image. But this essay is not just a biography of this painting—it is about the harshly critical response from a New York critic and friend who attacked its technique and intention, going so far as to reject it as political propaganda. Shahn admitted that *Allegory* "is an idea painting. It is also a highly emotional painting, and I hope that it is still primarily an image, a paint image." With great eloquence he explained that painting (like design) is not a limited medium. "Painting can contain the politician in a Daumier, the insurgent in a Goya, the suppliant in a Masaccio."

There are many who say design should stick to serving the client and designers should keep politics out of what they do. For anyone who wants to read an inspiring account of why this is a short-sighted view, I highly recommend "Biography of a Painting" as a way to trigger this charged conversation.

---

Originally published as "Something to Read This Summer, Or Now!" in *Design Observer*, June 5, 2017.

# DISCUSSION POINTS

- Why do artists write?
- How is a drawing or painting decoded?
- Should art and design be examined and analyzed to understand their meaning?
- Can art and design contain different points of view?

# ONE: DESIGN LANGUAGE

*When* EYE *magazine first published this now-bruising essay, I used the word "ugly" as a value and measure applied to graphic design and design education. My views of art history, pop culture, and recent design trends were considered herein about style and its meaning in graphic design. This essay has been reprinted in various outlets and talked about in schools. Since the 1990s, attitudes about ugliness and beauty have changed. However, this remains an essay that influenced the moment, the merits of which I encourage students to read and debate in this moment.*

# Cult of the Ugly

"Ask a toad what is beauty. . . . He will answer that it is a female with two great round eyes coming out of her little head, a large flat mouth, a yellow belly and a brown back" (Voltaire, *Philosophical Dictionary*, 1794). Ask Paul Rand what is beauty and he will answer that "the separation of form and function, of concept and execution, is not likely to produce objects of aesthetic value" (Paul Rand, *A Designer's Art*, 1985). Then ask the same question of the Cranbrook Academy of Art students who created the ad hoc desktop publication *Output* (1992), and judging by the evidence they might answer that beauty is chaos born of found letters layered on top of random patterns and shapes. Those who value functional simplicity would argue that the Cranbrook students' publication, like a toad's warts, is ugly. The difference is that unlike the toad, the Cranbrook students have deliberately given themselves the warts.

*Output* is eight unbound pages of blips, type fragments, random words, and other graphic minutiae purposefully given the serendipitous look of a printer's makeready. The lack of any explanatory précis (and only this end note: "Upcoming Issues From: School of the Art Institute of Chicago [and] University of Texas") leaves the reader confused as to its purpose or meaning, though its form leads one to presume that it is intended as a design manifesto, another "experiment" in the current plethora of aesthetically questionable graphic output. Given the increase in graduate school programs which provide both a laboratory setting and freedom from professional responsibility, the word "experiment" has to justify a multitude of sins.

The value of design experiments should not of course be measured only by what succeeds, since failures are often steps toward new discoveries. Experimentation is the engine of progress, its fuel a mixture of instinct, intelligence, and discipline. This is the case with certain of the graphic design experiments that have emanated from graduate schools in the US and Europe in recent years, work driven by instincts and obscured by theory, with ugliness its foremost by-product.

How is "ugly" to be defined in the current postmodern climate where existing systems are up for reevaluation, order is under attack, and the forced collision of disparate forms is the rule? For the moment, let us say that ugly design, as opposed to classical design (where adherence to the golden mean and a preference for balance and harmony serve as the foundation for even the most unconventional compositions), is the layering of inharmonious graphic forms in a way that results in confusing messages. By this definition, *Output* could be considered a prime example of ugliness in the service of fashionable experimentation. Though not intended to function in the commercial world, it was distributed to thousands of practicing designers on the American Institute of Graphic Arts and American Center for Design mailing lists, so rather than remain cloistered and protected from criticism as on-campus "research," it is a fair subject for scrutiny. It can legitimately be described as representing the current cult of ugliness.

The layered images, vernacular hybrids, low-resolution reproductions, and cacophonous blends of different types and letters at once challenge prevailing aesthetic beliefs and propose alternative paradigms. Like the output of communications rebels of the past (whether 1920s Futurists or 1960s psychedelic artists), this work demands that the viewer or reader accept nontraditional formats, which at best guide the eye for a specific purpose through a range of nonlinear "pathways," and at worst result in confusion.

But the reasons behind this wave are dubious. Does the current social and cultural condition involve the kind of upheaval to which critical ugliness is a time-honored companion? Or in the wake of earlier, more serious experimentation, has ugliness simply been assimilated into popular culture and become a stylish conceit?

The current wave began in the mid-1970s with the English punk scene, a raw expression of youth frustration manifested through shocking dress, music, and art. Punk's naive graphic language—an aggressive rejection of rational typography that echoes Dada and Futurist work—influenced designers in the late 1970s who seriously tested the limits imposed by modernist formalism. Punk's violent demeanor surfaced in Swiss, American, Dutch, and French design and spread to the mainstream in the form of a "new wave," or what American punk artist Gary Panter has called "sanitized punk." A key anti-canonical approach later called Swiss Punk—which in comparison with the gridlocked Swiss International Style was menacingly chaotic, though rooted in its own logic—was born in the mecca of rationalism, Basel, during the late 1970s. The modernist elders who were threatened (and offended) by the onslaught of Swiss Punk attacked it not so much because of its appearance, but because it symbolized the demise of modernist hegemony.

Ugly design can be a conscious attempt to create and define alternative standards. Like war paint, the dissonant styles which many contemporary designers have applied to their visual communications are meant to shock an enemy—complacency—as well as to encourage new reading and viewing patterns. The work of American designer Art Chantry combines the shock-and-educate approach with a concern for appropriateness. For over a decade Chantry has been creating eye-catching, low-budget graphics for the Seattle punk scene by using found commercial artifacts from industrial merchandise catalogs as key elements in his posters and flyers. While these "unsophisticated" graphics may be horrifying to designers who prefer

# *Ugly design can be a conscious attempt to create and define alternative standards.*

Shaker functionalism to punk vernacular, Chantry's design is decidedly functional within its context. Chantry's clever manipulations of found "art" into accessible, though unconventional, compositions prove that using ostensibly ugly forms can result in good design.

Postmodernism inspired a debate in graphic design in the mid-1970s by revealing that many perceptions of art and culture were one-dimensional. Postmodernism urgently questioned certainties laid down by modernism and rebelled against grand Eurocentric narratives in favor of multiplicity. The result in graphic design was to strip modernist formality of both its infrastructure and its outer covering. The grid was demolished, while neoclassical and contemporary ornament, such as dots, blips, and arrows, replaced the tidiness of the canonical approach. As in most artistic revolutions, the previous generation was attacked, while the generations before were curiously rehabilitated. The visual hallmarks of this rebellion, however, were inevitably reduced to stylistic mannerisms which forced even more radical experimentation. Extremism gave rise to fashionable ugliness as a form of nihilistic expression.

In "Ode on a Grecian Urn" (1819), the Romantic poet John Keats wrote the famous lines: "Beauty is truth, truth beauty,—that is all/Ye know on earth, and all ye need to know." Yet in today's environment, one standard of beauty is no more the truth than is one standard of ugliness. It is possible that the most convention-busting graphic design by students and alumni of Cranbrook, CalArts, and Rhode Island School of Design, among other hothouses where theoretical constructs are used to justify what the untutored eye might deem ugly, could become the foundation for new standards based on contemporary

*… while modernism smoothed out the rough edges of communications by prescribing a limited number of options, it also created a recipe for mediocrity.*

sensibilities. Certainly, these approaches have attracted many followers throughout the deign world.

"Where does beauty begin and where does it end?" wrote John Cage in *Silence* (1961). "Where it ends is where the artist begins." So in order to stretch the perimeters of art and design to any serious extent, it becomes necessary to suspend popular notions of beauty so that alternative aesthetic standards can be explored. This concept is essential to an analysis of a recent work by the Chicago company Segura, who designed the program/announcement for the 1993 *How* magazine Creative Vision conference and whose work represents the professional wing of the hothouse sensibility. Compared to the artless *Output*, Segura's seemingly anarchic booklet is an artfully engineered attempt to direct the reader through a maze of mundane information. Yet while the work might purport to confront complacency, it often merely obstructs comprehension.

A compilation of variegated visuals, the *How* piece is a veritable primer of cultish extremes at once compelling for its ingenuity yet undermined by its superficiality. Like a glutton, Segura has stuffed itself with all the latest conceits (including some of its own concoction) and has regurgitated them onto the pages. At first the juxtapositions of discordant visual material appear organic, but in fact little is left to chance. The result is a catalog of disharmony in the service of contemporaneity, an artifact that is already ossifying into a 1990s design style. It is a style that presumes that more is hipper than less, confusion is better than simplicity, fragmentation is smarter then continuity, and that ugliness is its own reward.

But is it possible that the surface might blind one to the inner beauty (i.e., intelligence) of this work? Ralph Waldo Emerson, in *The Conduct of*

*Life* (1860), wrote: "The secret of ugliness consists not in irregularity, but in being uninteresting." Given Emerson's measure, it could be argued that design is only ugly when devoid of aesthetic or conceptual forethought—for example, generic restaurant menus, store signs, and packages. Perhaps, then, the *How* booklet, which is drowning in forethought, should be "read" on a variety of levels wherein beauty and ugliness are mitigated by context and purpose. Perhaps—but given the excesses in this work, the result can only be described as a catalog of pretense.

During the late 1940s and 1950s, the modernist mission was to develop design systems that would protect the global (not just corporate) visual environment from blight. Yet while modernism smoothed out the rough edges of communications by prescribing a limited number of options, it also created a recipe for mediocrity. If a modernist design system is followed by rote, the result can be as uninteresting and therefore as ugly—according to Emerson's standard—as any non-designed newsletter or advertisement. So design that aggressively challenge the senses and intellect rather than following the pack should in theory be tolerated, if not encouraged.

For a new generation's ideas of good design—and beauty—to be challenged by its forerunners is, of course, a familiar pattern. Paul Rand, when criticized as one of those "Bauhaus boys" by American type master W. A. Dwiggins in the late 1930s, told an interviewer that he had always respected Dwiggins's work, "so why couldn't he see the value of what we were doing?" Rudy VanderLans, whose clarion call of the "new typography," *Emigre*, has been vituperatively criticized by Massimo Vignelli, has not returned the fire, but rather countered that he admires Vignelli's work despite his own interest in exploring alternatives made possible by new technologies. It could be argued that the language invented by Rand's "Bauhaus boys" challenged contemporary aesthetics in much the same way as VanderLans is doing in *Emigre* today. Indeed, VanderLans and those designers whom *Emigre* celebrates for their inventions—including Cranbrook alumni Edward Fella, Jeffery Keedy, and Allen Hori—are promoting new ways of making and seeing typography. The difference is that Rand's method was based strictly on ideas of balance and harmony which hold up under close scrutiny even today. The new young Turks, by

*...the line that separates parody and seriousness is thin, and the result is ugliness.*

contrast, reject such verities in favor of imposed discordance and disharmony, which might be rationalized as personal expression, but not as viable visual communication, and so in the end will be a blip (or tangent) in the continuum of graphic design history.

Edward Fella's work is a good example. Fella began his career as a commercial artist, became a guest critic at Cranbrook, and later enrolled as a graduate student, imbuing in other students an appreciation for the naïf (or folk) traditions of commercial culture. He "convincingly deployed highly personal art-based imagery and typography in his design for the public," explains Lorraine Wild in her essay "Transgression and Delight: Graphic Design at Cranbrook" (*Cranbrook Design: The New Discourse*, 1990). He also introduced what Wild describes as "the vernacular, the impure, the incorrect, and all the other forbidden excesses" to his graduate studies. These excesses, such as nineteenth-century fat faces, comical stock printers' cuts, ornamental dingbats, hand scrawls, and out-of-focus photographs, were anathema to the early modernists, who had battled to expunge such eyesores from public view.

Similar forms had been used prior to the 1980s in a more sanitized way by American designers such as Phil Gips in *Monocle* magazine, Otto Storch in *McCall's* magazine, and Bea Feitler in *Ms.* magazine. For these designers, novelty job printers' typefaces and rules were not just crass curios employed as affectations, but appropriate components of stylish layouts. While they provided an alternative to the cold, systematic typefaces favored by the International Style, they appeared in compositions that were nonetheless clean and accessible. These were not experiments, but "solutions" to design problems.

Two decades later, Fella too reemployed many of the typically ugly novelty typefaces as well as otherwise neutral canonical letterforms, which he stretched and distorted to achieve purposefully artless effects for use on gallery and exhibition announcements. Unlike Gips's and Feitler's work, these were aggressively unconventional. In *Cranbrook Design: The New Discourse*, Fella's challenges to "normal" expectations of typography are described as ranging from "low parody to high seriousness." But the line that separates parody and seriousness is thin, and the result is ugliness. As a critique of the slick design practiced throughout corporate culture, Fella's work is not without a certain acerbity. As personal research, indeed as personal art, it can be justified, but as a model for commercial practice, this kind of ugliness is a dead end.

"Just maybe, a small independent graduate program is precisely where such daunting research and invention in graphic design should occur," argues Wild. And one would have to agree that given the strictures of the marketplace, it is hard to break meaningful ground while serving a client's needs and wants. Nevertheless, the marketplace can provide important safeguards—Rand, for example, never had the opportunity to experiment outside the business arena and since he was ostensibly self-taught, virtually everything he invented was "on the job." Jeffery Keedy and Allen Hori, both of whom had a modicum of design experience before attending Cranbrook, availed themselves of the luxury of experimenting free of marketplace demands. For them, graduate school was a place to test out ideas that "transgressed" as far as possible from accepted standards. So Wild is correct in her assertion that it is better to do research and development in a dedicated and sympathetic atmosphere. But such an atmosphere can also be polluted by its own freedoms.

The ugly excesses—or Frankenstein's little monsters like *Output*—are often exhibited in public to promulgate "the new design discourse." In fact, they merely further the cause of ambiguity and ugliness. Since graduate school hothouses push their work into the real world, some of what is purely experimental is accepted by neophytes as a viable model, and students, being students, will inevitably misuse it. Who can blame them if their mentors are doing so, too?

Common to all graphic designers practicing in the current wave is the self-indulgence that informs some of the worst experimental fine art. But what ultimately derails much of this work is what critic Dugald Stermer calls "adults making kids' drawings." When Art Chantry uses naive or ugly design elements, he transforms them into viable tools. Conversely, Jeffery Keedy's Lushus, a bawdy shove-it-in-your-face novelty typeface, is taken seriously by some and turns up on printed materials (such as the Dutch *Best Book Designs* cover) as an affront to, not a parody of, typographic standards. When the layered, vernacular look is practiced in the extreme, whether with forethought or not, it simply contributes to the perpetuation of bad design.

"Rarely has beauty been an end in itself," wrote Paul Rand in *Paul Rand: A Designer's Art*. And it is equally mistaken to treat ugliness as an end result in itself. Ugliness is valid, even refreshing, when it is key to an indigenous language representing alternative ideas and cultures. The problem with the cult of ugly graphic design emanating from the major design academies and their alumni is that it has so quickly become a style that appeals to anyone without the intelligence, discipline, or good sense to make something more interesting out of it. While the proponents are following their various muses, their followers are misusing their signature designs and typography as style without substance. Ugliness as a tool, a weapon, even as a code is not a problem when it is a result of form following function. But ugliness as its own virtue—or as a knee-jerk reaction to the status quo—diminishes all design.

Originally published in *EYE* magazine, issue no. 9, Summer 1993.

## DISCUSSION POINTS

- Is the concept of ugliness a valid principle to use in discussions of graphic design and typography?

- What does "ugly" mean in today's design vocabulary?

- What would be the guiding critique of design in the current age?

- Can design be criticized using a universal standard?

# The Legibility Wars

"What did you do during the Legibility Wars?" asked one of my more inquisitive design history students.

"Well, it wasn't actually a war," I said, recalling the period during the mid-1980s through the mid- to late 1990s when there were stark divisions between new and old design generations—the young anti-modernists, and the established followers of modernism. "It was rather a skirmish between a bunch of young designers, like your age now, who were called New Wave, Postmodern, Swiss Punk, whatever, and believed it necessary to reject the status quo for something freer and more contemporary. Doing that meant criticizing old-guard designers, who believed design should be simple—clean on tight grids and Helveticized."

"Do you mean bland?" he quizzed further.

"Maybe some of it was bland," I conceded. "But it was more like a new generation was feeling its oats and it was inevitable." New technology was making unprecedented options possible. Aesthetic standards were changing because young designers wanted to try everything, while the older designers, especially the devout modern ones, believed everything had already been tried.

"I read that Massimo Vignelli called a lot of the new digital and retro stuff 'garbage,'" my student said. "What did you say or do about it back then?"

"I was more or less on the modernist side and wrote about it in a 1993 *EYE* magazine essay called 'Cult of the Ugly.'" I wasn't against illegibility per se, just the stuff that seemed to be done badly. I justified biased distinctions not between beautiful and ugly, but between good ugly and bad ugly, or what was done with an experimental rationale and with merely style and fashion as the motive.

As I wrote in *EYE* at the time, "Ugly design can be a conscious attempt to create and define alternative standards. Like war paint, the dissonant styles which many contemporary designers have applied to their visual communications are meant to shock an enemy—complacency—as well as to encourage new reading and viewing patterns." To make my point, I cited Art Chantry. "[His work] combines the shock-and-educate approach with a concern for appropriateness. For over a decade Chantry has been creating eye-catching, low-budget graphics for the Seattle punk scene by using found commercial artifacts from industrial merchandise catalogs as key elements in his posters and flyers. While these 'unsophisticated' graphics may be horrifying to designers who prefer Shaker functionalism to punk vernacular, Chantry's design is decidedly functional within its context. Chantry's clever manipulations of found 'art' into accessible, though unconventional, compositions prove that using ostensibly ugly forms can result in good design."

"So you were a reactionary?" my student probed.

"I guess so," I responded, slightly annoyed. "But you had to understand the times." The modernists were fighting for their principles in academic articles and seminars, but mostly among themselves. I was caught up on both sides, but chose to go on record against the larger problem of illegibility, which

*...the Legibility Wars are indeed part of our collective graphic design history—an encapsulation of a defining (or, more aptly, redefining) moment when the scales shifted toward the new digital era.*

I defined as ugly. Later, I surrendered to the forces of inevitability and the realization that there was no war to be won, no battle to be fought or skirmish to be had. There was no getting around the fact that newly developed—and newly available—technology would stimulate new ways of doing things.

"Other than a few designers," he asked, "did anyone care?"

"I don't know," I muttered. "Not too many 'anyones' care about graphic design other than those of us who are involved, anyway." While many may have forgotten them today, the Legibility Wars are indeed part of our collective graphic design history—an encapsulation of a defining (or, more aptly, redefining) moment when the scales shifted toward the new digital era. And that's why I'm writing this personal reexamination of what the legibility skirmish was all about, where it ended up, and what, if anything, it means to practitioners, teachers, and scholars today.

## Defining the Era

Modernism in the 1920s was a revolution that replaced outmoded traditions with radical methods of producing art, architecture, design, music, dance,

*On the whole, legibility is not the same as readability. The sin is not in breaking the former but in breaking the latter.*

and literature inspired by science and technology—as well as psychology. We still admire its collective output and celebrate it in countless exhibits and books. Collage, asymmetrical typography, and anarchic layouts were raw and exciting—a new language. But ultimately the next evolution, Swiss Modernism, was hijacked for political and institutional uses. The modernist vocabulary became a means of communication to and from the global corporate world in the 1960s, which gave way to modernistic styling. The Swiss style's characteristics included very readable sans serif type, generous amounts of white space, geometry, and an emphasis on simplicity. It ran the gamut from the exquisite to the bland. It was the formulaic side of the equation that was being critiqued by a new generation who believed design had to have more flexibility than flush-left Helvetica and serve more than just corporate identities. So in 1984, when Apple's first TV commercial announced that the Macintosh was the next major design tool, young creatives embraced its power, in part to make use of primitive techniques like pixelating, overlapping, under-printing, and serendipitous digital flaws. Illegibility was a flaw turned into a code used by 1980s graphic designers just like psychedelia was for 1960s poster artists. Designers were also being a tad sadistic—like cats playing with mice, illegibility was like batting around modernists before the kill.

On the whole, legibility is not the same as readability. The sin is not in breaking the former but in breaking the latter. It can be argued that when something is illegible it is unreadable, but in fact, it is readable for those who crack the code. In the early 1920s, Dada and surrealist typography broke many of the classical rules of printing, but could be read by anyone with the patience to solve the puzzles or pass roadblocks to unfettered comprehension.

In the mid-1980s and '90s, Rudy VanderLans's *Emigre* magazine, the voice of the new type and digital typography movement, was dedicated to showcasing a coterie of avid contra-modernists who railed against dead style in favor of a so-called postmodern, or PoMo, approach that, in part, questioned the very form and function of type and imagery and the role played by the grid in making type read well. Again, illegibility was only a small part of the questions and answers. But altering these standards often meant taking license both in practice and in theory. Katherine McCoy, who ran Cranbrook Academy's graphic design program, saw this legibility/readability construct as part of a linguistic evolution: "Visual phenomena are analyzed as language encoded for meaning. Meanings are deconstructed, exposing the dynamics of power and the manipulation of meaning." This played out in the more experimental design schools and programs that gave students permission to see how far illegibility could be pushed before incompressibility set in.

Illegibility, such as it was, showed up in *Emigre* and in niche magazines like David Carson's *Ray Gun* and *Speak*, *Shift*, *Blur*, and *Lava*, among others. But even the complex layering of type, pictures, and doodads that gave an impression of illegibility was never entirely so. (In a more extreme example, David Carson set an entire *Ray Gun* in dingbats rather than type—but the text was still published in the back of the magazine.) For those who had no patience for deciphering, if it wasn't clean, it was considered illegible.

With Rick Poynor's first *Typography Now* book (Edward Booth Clibborn Editions, 1991), the question about whether or not what was taking place was a legitimate type revolution was answered. There was enough "new typography" to prove real generational movement. In 1997, I made my own contribution with *Faces on the Edge* (coauthored with Anne Fink, Van Nostrand Rinehold). Poynor's *Typography Now Two: Implosion* (1998) curiously brought closure to the illegibility debate, since even the most radical were readable. And his *No More Rules: Graphic Design and Postmodernism* (2003) summed up the whole phenomenon as a complete historical epoch from 1980 to 2000. In fact, illegibility had stopped being a defining postmodern issue years before the last regular issue of *Emigre* (#69) was published in 2005.

## Reading Between the Lines

The real revolution was technology, which also had the effect of starkly increasing the power of women in design—and the number of women experimenting with illegibility and readability was considerable. April Greiman had been entrenched in modernism until 1984, when she embraced the first Macintosh with gusto. While most graphic designers were skeptical or afraid of its mystery, Greiman established herself as the pioneer—specifically of the digital commingling collage of video and still photography with type. Mixed media played a role in how text was composed and rendered legible or illegible, and Greiman's work was called New Wave in the design press while it defied all imposed labels. "[She] had been rocking the Modernist boat for a few years when she undertook a major assault upon the design community's sensibilities and preconceptions of what constitutes design," the AIGA stated in 1998 when it awarded her its Lifetime Medal of Achievement. The incident in question? In 1986 Greiman was the subject and designer of *Design Quarterly* #133. It was an opportunity not only to present her digital work to the world, "but to ask a larger question of the work and the medium: Does it make sense? Reading Wittgenstein on the topic, she identified with his conclusion: 'It makes sense if you give it sense,'" noted the AIGA. Illegibility was simply an outcome of other perceptual experiments. Greiman trashed the standard thirty-two-page format of *Design Quarterly*, and instead created a poster that folded out to almost three by six feet. On the front was a pixelated image of Greiman's naked body amid layers of text and image; the poster also included notations on the digital process, and the whole thing was composed on the Macintosh using MacDraw. "Beyond considering whether digital technologies made sense, the *Design Quarterly* poster seemed to embody the disillusionment of a nation deeply wounded by the Vietnam War and shaped by the growth of feminism, spiritualism, Eastern religion, Jungian archetypes and dream symbolism," the AIGA wrote.

While completely readable, Greiman did not make it easy on purpose. She showed that illegibility simply needed translation—and when translated, the power was apparent.

Elsewhere, digital typeface design was a significant postmodern outlier, and no one captured the essence and evolution of the 1980s and '90s better than Zuzana Licko, the creator of such early digital fonts as Lo-Res and Matrix. Dozens of her faces, both precise and grungy, classical and novel, helped to typographically define graphic design that can in some instances pinpoint postmodern's moment of conception and in others, like Mr and Mrs Eaves, have the timeless look that defies the stereotypes and clichés of either "-ism." This type was not illegible. It was type! Type is legible by definition. Users could do whatever they pleased with it. And while some layered and distorted it, others used it straight up and easily readable. The fact that messages needed to be read was never a question. Only how they'd be read was of concern—and who would read them. I contend the illegibility skirmish was about designers talking to other designers. It was a natural outgrowth of a profession in transition.

Today, all kinds of design theatrics coexist separately or together. Rather than one or two dominant styles, there are multiple personalities in graphic design, and a lot more on digital screens. The experimental versus classical discourse may occasionally flare up—as will the difference between readability and legibility—but the polarization that spiced up the earlier argument is over. In its wake is the sense that graphic designers are freer from hard-and-fast rules, but rarely is the issue more radical than that. "The truth is," I told my design history students, "making type and typography more readable was ultimately more useful to old and young designers alike than making it less so." Most clients would agree.

Originally published as "The Legibility Wars of the '80s and '90s" in *Print* magazine, Fall 2016.

## DISCUSSION POINTS

- What is the difference between legibility and readability?
- Must all type and typography be clear and clean?
- Why are there so many different typefaces?
- Do typefaces express emotion?

*This essay was written a number of years after "Cult of the Ugly." Post-nostalgia stress disorder for the 1990s (a curious love/hate relationship with grunge type) ended as 2000 came to a close. This was written when the time had come for design pundits to start looking forward to see what could be learned from the period of anarchic design.*

# The Decade of Dirty Design

The millennium began tumultuously with the contested election of George W. Bush. The nation was in fairly good economic health owing to the surpluses accrued by the Clinton administration, and graphic design was rolling merrily along with plenty of work for everyone. Stylistically, designers had just emerged from a period of hyper-experimentation that pitted old modernist verities, such as order and clarity, against computer-driven chaos, which some called postmodern and others (myself included) sarcastically referred to as "ugly." Yet from a more sympathetic and reasoned perspective, "The early '90s was an extraordinarily fertile period," wrote Ellen Lupton recently at Printmag.com (http://www.printmag.com/Article/Typography-in-the-1990s). "In the U.S., a far-flung vanguard had spread out from Cranbrook and CalArts, where several generations of designers—from Ed Fella to Elliott Earls—had embraced formal experimentation as a mode of critical inquiry. *Emigre* magazine, edited and art directed by Rudy VanderLans, provided an over-scaled paper canvas for experimental layout, writing, and typeface design." And let's not forget David Carson's stinging jabs at typographic propriety. He significantly influenced a generation to embrace typography as an expressive medium.

No matter which side of the aesthetic or philosophical divide one was on, this was a critically exciting time to be a graphic designer. Although the computer was the dominant medium, during the early 1990s designers were transitioning from the hand to the pixel, experiencing all the visual quirks and anomalies that came with technological unease. By the end of the decade and the beginning of the twenty-first century, despite the Y2K-end-of-civilization hoopla, the computer was firmly entrenched in the lives of designers, and there was not only an aesthetic calming down, but a frenetic media migration. Designers were not only relying on the computer for clean, crisp, and flaw-free print work, they were turning from the printed page to video, audio, and other motion and sound formats.

Mastery of the computer's options meant by the end of the twentieth century a new generation of designers were able to do much more than merely command Illustrator, Quark, and Photoshop programs—they had figured out how to wed technique to concept, and to produce design that often had an exterior life other than the client's message. The earlier grungy experimentation gave way to a new clarity and rationalism—even a new minimalism began to take hold with the return to Helvetica and other emblematic sans serif faces.

So arguably, neo-modernism of the kind practiced in, say, *Wallpaper** magazine was the defining style of the decade. But actually that was not the case. Eclecticism was still in force, and while some designers were out-of-the-closet modernists, others followed an Expressionist model. (You want names? Just look at the AIGA Graphic Design Archive for the evidence.) But eclecticism is too broad a notion to be a decade-defining style. The 1990s was clearly the digital decade, with all that that represents—an evolution from embracing digital mistakes to practicing digital precision. Axiomatically, generations challenge one another. If the 1990s is devoutly digital, then the 2000s should be the "anti-digital decade."

Where's the proof, Mr. Pundit? Anecdotally, I point to the rationales from various students entering the MFA Designer as Author program I cochair (with Lita Talarico). When the first wave of students, who entered the program from the late 1990s through the mid-2000s, were asked why they signed up, the answer was "To get back to the hand." Now, this does not mean a total rejection of the computer (for that would be professional suicide), but it does mean that the craft aspect of design was lacking in their formal educations and practices. With the increase of the DIY sensibility, with renewed emphasis on "making things from scratch," designers were feeling a need to make physical (not virtual) contact with their materials and outcomes. It is no surprise that sewing and scrapbooking emerged as popular hobbies, but it was somewhat novel that they were integrated into the graphic design practice.

Over the past five years, I coauthored three books that support this "anti-digital" claim: *Handwritten* (with Mirko Ilic), *New Vintage Type*, and *New Ornamental Type* (with Gail Anderson). The first is totally focused on typography done by the original ten digits (although unavoidably it was scanned into a computer). The other two books revisit older styles and eras, and a good amount of the material is generated by hand with a DIY underpinning. Consistent with this assertion, hand typesetting, letterpress printing, and silkscreen techniques are on the rise in schools and workshops. And speaking of workshops, a former MFA Designer as Author student created, as a thesis, a workshop titled Dirty Weekend (www.dirty-weekend.org), a series of three weekend sessions that focus exclusively on painting, carving, cutting, and printing by hand. At the time, workshop attendees at various venues in New York proved that the hand is at least as mighty as the pixel.

Why call this anti-digital? Isn't it just an alternative to the dominant medium, but certainly not a substitute for it? Perhaps. But since pundits like to sum up moments—especially decades—for purposes of further debate I will refer to this as "The Decade of Dirty Design" until someone proves otherwise.

---

Originally published on *AIGA VOICE*, December 9, 2009.

# DISCUSSION POINTS

- Did "ugly design" actually have meaning for designers?

- Design styles are subject to market acceptance. If dirty design sold products, would it have survived?

- Is dirty design an actual stylistic category?

- Is this approach to design still evident in the commercial world today?

*The clash between modernism and postmodernism (aka PM or PoMo) triggered a seismic shift in culture, particularly in art and design, during the final third of the twentieth century. It also caused plenty of confusion as to what PM actually represented—ideology or style, neither or both.*

# The PoMo Brouhaha

With graphic design, PoMo was less quake than natural transformation—as in pop music from, say, the era of big bands and young Frank Sinatra to rock 'n' roll and the Beatles. In other words, a generational adjustment in popular taste influenced by everything from aesthetics to technology to marketing. The modern vs. postmodern brouhaha wasn't nearly as cataclysmic as during the early twentieth century, before the real modern revolution had lost steam, when kindred antiestablishment movements known throughout Europe by their evocative names, like Vorticist, Futurist, Zenitist, Productionist, Dadaist, etc., were lumped together under a single modernist banner. Modernism was the comet that wiped out the dinosaurs. Yet it gave way to rote modernistic styling, notably in advertising and graphic design, which made postmodernism inevitable.

Postmodernism began in architecture as critiques by disillusioned modernists that quickly spread to other disciplines during the late 1970s and developed into a process. PM rejected Bauhausian rigidity and geometric precision for more fluid, sensual, alluring forms, including the reintroduction of ornament and ostentatious space, spiced sometimes with a bit of self-mocking wit. Paradoxically, Bauhaus-inspired architecture became the epitome of corporate identification. Modernism's potential to enliven advertising and editorial genres was incalculable. World War II, however, put a full stop to experimental modernism, and when the war was over, modernism's priorities were commerce-oriented.

Postmodernism's impact on graphic design and vice versa was inconsequential (or invisible) at first because modernism was (and still is) widely practiced in its mid-century or "late" form. Even today the two isms share some common traits.

In the late 1940s through the early '60s, during the periods of abstract expressionism, pop and op art, the International Style (or Swiss School) of graphic design, known for its elemental economy and typographic rigidity, inherited the Bauhaus mantle after the war. Taught in the fifties at the Kunstgewerbeschule in Zürich and Schule für Gestaltung Basel, the epicenters of modern practice, the pedagogy stretched far beyond its borders, to Yale in New Haven, Philadelphia University of the Arts, Illinois Institute of Technology (New Bauhaus), and other American art colleges. The primary visual characteristics included sans serif type (primarily Akizenz Grotesque, Helvetica, and Univers), generous amounts of white space, geometric iconography, and high-contrast photography.

Yet even Swiss-inspired modernism did not come from a mold. Distinct attributes defined certain nations and their respective designers. American modernists, among them Paul Rand, Lester Beall, Saul Bass, Bradbury Thompson, and others, allowed playful instincts to emerge. Even a devout European modernist who escaped from the Nazis to the United States, Ladislav Sutnar, often balanced on the edge of modernist practice with something akin to proto-postmodernism. There was so much room for personal expression in the US that it is still easy to confuse certain of these designers' works as a prelude to postmodernism.

Where the two approaches merged to create hybrids, look no further than the incipient neo-modern insurgences that prevailed during the 1960s in Eastern Europe. Through the introduction of conceptual thinking, surreal illustration, and expressive lettering, Iron Curtain bloc nations like Poland, Czechoslovakia, and Hungary, among others, were hotbeds for innovative cultural, film, theater, and art posters that both echoed and diverged from Western European modernism. Work by Polish designers Henryk Tomaszewski, Roman Cieslewicz, and Czech Zdeněk Ziegler, among others, were respected by admiring Westerners through the feature articles in Zurich-based *Graphis* magazine, edited by Walter Herdeg. This new eclecticism gave credibility to vintage and retro typefaces, which were anathema to modernists.

Graphic design is a barometer of commercial styles and fashions and the ups and downs of modernist and postmodernist approaches. Postmodernism did not entirely supplant modernism but coincided with and sometimes smashed into it—and, like atoms in a collider, produced another, sometimes explosive style.

Postmodernism occurred in the mid-1980s, when Tibor Kalman, founder of New York–based M & Co., began designing with so-called vernacular or untutored forms (the tasteless stuff that drove modernists out of their skins), like Chinese menu design, as a means of protesting what he called an elitist modernistic professionalism. He did not call himself postmodern, but railed against corporate modernism: "[M]y overall worry about the design business is whether as a group we are becoming overly influenced by money and professional success," he argued in a 2011 debate sponsored by *Print* magazine, "and whether that's impinging on our ability to criticize our clients and make an impact on the world and as a group influence culture."[1]

The corporate system that modernism served was indeed being critiqued by a new generation of designers who believed design was integral to social good on the one hand while making new mass visual ideas come alive on the other. That is one reason why, when Apple's 1984 TV commercial announced

---

[1]  Aaron Kenedi, "Tibor Kalman vs. Joe Duffy Revisited," *Print*, April 6, 2011, http://www.printmag.com/interviews/tibor-kalman-vs-joe-duffy-a-retrospective.

that the Macintosh was the next major design tool, fearless designers went computer-crazy. The power of the computer implied power for designers and signaled new opportunities for postmodernizing design through the serendipity of primitive techniques like pixelating, overlapping, under-printing, and serendipitous digital flaws that were de rigueur. The new digital tools, which actually ensured the precision of crisp, gridlocked modernist formats, were boons for postmodernists to play with illegibility and engage in other typographical sins against propriety and beauty.

Postmodernism, which even the curators of the 2011 exhibition at the V&A, *Postmodernism: Style and Subversion, 1970–1990*, refused to categorically define,[2] was insinuated into graphic design long before the term was coined. Modernism and postmodernism could (and perhaps should) be seen as graphic styles that at once contradict and play off and with one another. Setting aside for a moment PoMo theory and pedagogy of the 1980s and '90s, even in the late 1940s and '50s modernists battled against renegades who rejected and ignored the changes in design form that modern designers had accomplished. But the battle lines were sometimes blurry. Paul Rand was a devoted form-follows-function modernist who made photo collage and cut paper illustrations that might seem postmodern today by more rigid Swiss colleagues. Although his design was not as risqué as that of, say, Neville Brody, April Greiman, or David Carson, he did not always strictly adhere to minimalism. Dan Friedman, who studied at ULM School, a hotbed of orthodox modernism, and later at Schule für Gestaltung Basel of Design, with both the rebellious Wolfgang Weingart and modernist Armin Hofmann, called his later work "radical modernism"[3] because it contained eccentric visual traits and color play that later suggested a strain of postmodernism. Even earlier, late 1960s rock poster master Victor Moscoso, who studied with modernist guru Josef Albers at Yale, ignored all the modern rules of form and function in what could arguably be called postmodern—but it was called psychedelic. And of course Push Pin Studios, first among the design/illustration studios in the 1950s and '60s, proudly rejected the sterility of

2   "Postmodernism," Victoria and Albert Museum, http://www.vam.ac.uk/page/p/postmodernism/.

3   Dan Friedman, *Radical Modernism*, https://www.amazon.com/Dan-Friedman-Radical-Modernism/dp/0300058489.

Swiss Modernism's limiting typo-pictorial guidelines. Their employ of historical graphic elements, including reinterpreted Victorian, art nouveau, and art deco, went totally against the grain of modernism. Milton Glaser and Seymour Chwast, Push Pin's cofounders, had proto-postmodernist leanings; Glaser admitted in an AIGA interview that they rejected "the strong authoritarianism of modernism."[4] Then there was Herb Lubalin, who became known for, among other things, smashed and overlapping typography that was resolutely contemporary but avoided modernist rigidity. His work was not postmodern, but today it might be so considered.

Asked to define modernism, Paul Rand said: "It means integrity; it means honesty; it means the absence of sentimentality and the absence of nostalgia; it means simplicity; it means clarity."[5] Postmodern, presumably was the opposite of all that. Yet the abovementioned Friedman, Moscoso, Lubalin, and Push Pin adhered to Rand's guidelines.

By the late 1980s and '90s, the new generation of PoMo designers finally had a soapbox. *Emigre* magazine, the voice of the new type and digital typography edited by Rudy VanderLans, was dedicated to showcasing a coterie of avid contra-modernists. In a 1995 story in *Emigre*, Jeffery Keedy decried Zombie Modernism as a walking dead style. But whatever was the next thing, postmodernism, New Wave, Newer Wave, etc., was an enigma. The curators of the V&A exhibition, Glenn Adamson and Jane Pavit, wrote: "The reader will not find anywhere in this book, or the exhibition it accompanies, a single handy definition of postmodernism." In his review of the exhibition in *EYE* magazine, design critic Rick Poynor wrote: "That doesn't mean that the book and (in a necessarily simpler way) the show avoid the issue—they offer many rewarding perspectives on the subject. But any attempt to reduce such an intricate set of cultural factors across so many kinds of art, design and media to a brief, all-encompassing definition would be a misrepresentation."[6]

[4]  Patrick Argent, "Milton Glaser," American Institute of Graphic Arts, http://www.aiga.org/medalist-miltonglaser/.

[5]  Interview with author at Cooper Union, November 1996.

[6]  Rick Poynor, "Did We Ever Stop Being Postmodern?" DesignObserver.com, October 16, 2011, http://designobserver.com/feature/did-we-ever-stop-being-postmodern/30798/.

Perhaps PoMo is not a philosophy or style, but a bracket, of sorts, around which is anything that does not fit or is contrary to the definition of modernism. Arguably, there is a lot of unintentional un-modern design spanning the period from 1970 to 2000. Punk, for instance, was a visceral approach that defied the rules of all proper design but was a slap in modernism's face in particular. It is rarely in the PoMo bucket, perhaps because it is not stylish or deliberate enough. Whereas what is sometimes called grunge, which is a lot like punk in terms of the defacement of classical design, is considered by some to be PM. The work by Art Chantry, the celebrated punk- and post-punk-era poster designer, falls in and out of PoMo because he often employs vernacular type and imagery that routinely bust the grid, and employs vintage stock art. He refuses to call himself postmodern, and if accepting of labels at all, he argues that graphic design is commercial folk art, so he is a folk artist. Stock cuts characterize the styles of Charles Spencer Anderson, who seized the monopoly on refined vintage commercial art clichés, which he refined and retrofitted. His work fits squarely into a retro style signaling a nostalgia anathema to orthodox modernism and leaning toward postmodernism.

Retro came into focus when Philip B. Meggs, the pioneering graphic design historian, wrote "The Women Who Saved New York."[7] Featured were four women, leaders of the retro "movement": Paula Scher, Louise Fili, Carin Goldberg, and the late Lorraine Louie. Each was dipping into design history for inspiration and reinterpreting it in a personal way. The story was important for two reasons: It focused on the rise of women and the fact that men had dominated the modernist field. It also supported the notion that retro was chronologically and aesthetically under a postmodern umbrella. Consequently, other postmodern women designers began to get publicity in the design press. Many, in fact, were modernist-trained designers who took turns toward postmodern aesthetics. Among the most visible, Deborah Sussman, who studied at the Chicago Bauhaus and worked at the Charles and Ray Eames Studio, designed the first postmodern graphic identity for the Los Angeles Olympics in 1984, filled with colors and patterns that some critics dubbed California Modern (aka postmodern).

[7] *Print* magazine, January/February 1989 (vol. 43, issue 1).

After working for Unimark, a decidedly male modernist studio (cofounded by modernist extraordinaire Massimo Vignelli), Kathy McCoy took over the graphic design department at Cranbrook Academy (accused by Vignelli of being one of the "most dangerous design schools" in the world), which was a wellspring of a large number of designers who helped define postmodern-deconstructive style. Influenced by architects Robert Venturi and Denise Scott-Brown's postmodernist theories, the study of semiotics and, later, post-structuralism and deconstruction from French literary movements, McCoy's work and teaching argued that "visual phenomena are analyzed as language encoded for meaning. Meanings are deconstructed, exposing the dynamics of power and the manipulation of meaning."[8] Cranbrook under McCoy was the theoretical sweet spot of generation PoMo.

It is important to realize that new technology increased the power of women in design, and the number of postmodern women at that. April Greiman was one of postmodern graphic design's key pioneers. A student of Weingart, she had been entrenched in modernism until 1984, when the first Macintosh was introduced. While most graphic designers were either reluctant to engage in or skeptical of the computer's potential creative force, Greiman took the leap of digital commingling collage of video and still photography with type. Her mixed media work was known as New Wave in the design press, but it also fell under the PoMo banner. "She had been rocking the Modernist boat for a few years when she undertook a major assault upon the design community's sensibilities and preconceptions of what constitutes design in 1986, in an issue of *Design Quarterly*," stated AIGA in 1998[9] when she received its Lifetime Medal of Achievement. Greiman was the subject and designer of *Design Quarterly* #133, published by the Walker Art Center. It was thus an opportunity not only to present her digital work, "but to ask a larger question of the work and the medium: Does it make sense? Reading Wittgenstein on the topic, she identified with his conclusion: 'It makes sense if you give it sense,'" noted the AIGA.

[8]  Katherine McCoy, "Thoughts on Design Writing," DesignTraveler, April 19, 2015, https://designtraveler.wordpress.com/2015/04/19/katherine-mccoy-thoughts-on-design-writing/.

[9]  Steven Heller, "April Greiman," American Institute of Graphic Arts, http://www.aiga.org/medalist-aprilgreiman/.

Her influence in multimedia design continues to have far-reaching implications for female and male designers.

Digital typeface design was a significant postmodern outlier, and no one captured the essence and evolution of the 1980s and '90s better than Zuzana Licko, the designer of such early digital fonts as Lo-Res, Citizen, and Matrix. "I'm sure that being free of preconceived notions regarding typeface design helped me in exploring this new medium to the fullest," Licko told *EYE* magazine.[10] "It's interesting how the gradual sophistication of my type design abilities has been matched by advances in the Apple Macintosh's capabilities, so it has continued to be the ideal tool for me." Dozens of her faces both precise and grungy, classical and novel, helped to typographically define graphic design that can in some instances pinpoint PoMo's moment of conception and in others, like Mr and Mrs Eaves, have the timeless look that defies the stereotypes and clichés of either ism.

Today, the banners still wave, but modern tenets and postmodern theatrics coexist, separately or together. Rather than one or two dominant styles, there are multiple personalities in graphic design, and a lot more on video and digital screens. Sinatra and the Beatles exist, so to speak, on the same iTunes playlists along with disco, punk, and hip-hop—as well as combinations of all and more. The modern vs. postmodern discourse may occasionally prompt a critical or theoretical debate—like the difference between readability and legibility—but the polarization that spiced up the earlier discourse is over. Yet, for the sake of history, hopefully not forgotten.

Originally published in *Post Modern Design Complete*, edited by Judith Gura (London: Thames & Hudson, 2017).

# DISCUSSION POINTS

- What defines PoMo graphic design?
- Is PoMo a style or a philosophy?
- Where does PoMo intersect with modernism?

[10] *EYE* no. 43, vol. 11, 2002.

*Vines and tendrils are strangling designed surfaces, the result of a decoration deficiency in the design diet or a natural tendency toward ornamentation. The cult of the squiggly has developed over the past decade with a few innovative form-givers seeding scores of exponents, ultimately spreading squiggly ornament that is alternately appropriate and nonsensical.*

# The Cult of the Squiggly

This is not the first time ornament has been so invasive.

An ornamental epidemic in the late nineteenth century prompted Austrian architect Adolf Loos to write a 1908 essay titled "Ornament and Crime." After the 1896 introduction of art nouveau and its offshoots, Jugendstil, Vienna Secession, Stile Liberty, and Modernista, floriated madness attacked everything from posters and typography to furniture and buildings. Loos wrote: "the evolution of culture marches with the elimination of ornament from useful objects." His preference for "smooth and precious surfaces" derived from a belief that functional objects swathed in ornament were guaranteed to become obsolete. Moreover, he believed that superfluous design was both a waste of time and immoral, too.

Yet barely twenty years later, just prior to the Great Depression, the strategy known as "forced obsolescence," what the American adman and design critic Earnest Elmo Calkins referred to as "styling the goods," was celebrated for having helped bring the United States economy back from material stagnation to consumerist vibrancy—in large part by adding ornament, like some sort of magic swaddling, to products and advertisements.

Visual austerity was viewed as puritanical. And who could argue that an ornamental Persian miniature, with its complex graphic layering, or *The Book of Kells*, with the interlocking and serpentine filigree that fill its pages, is not among the most beautiful of graphic artifacts? How could baroque or rococo motifs in print be indicted as crimes against the eye?

William Morris, the late-nineteenth-century English designer, printer, author, social critic, and founder of the Arts and Crafts movement, exalted in ornamentation. His design for the *Kelmscott Chaucer*, from its sumptuous ornamental borders to its decorative initial letters, proved to be the pinnacle of his career as a "graphic designer." But the *Kelmscott Chaucer* was more than simply a revival. It was the realization of Morris's belief that arts and crafts would counteract the corrosive impact of industrial pollution. Ornament was not a veil to hide ugly industrial wares—it was an antidote to the perceived poisons spewing from factory chimneys.

Ornament is not inherently evil, even in excessive doses. Nonetheless, passions are often inflamed when even the hint of ornamentation is injected into matters of modern design. The Bauhaus rejected ornamentation as symptomatic of a bourgeois aesthetic disorder. Followers of orthodox modernism, even to this day, maintain that minimalism enables clear communication—purity is transcendent. They rail against what in the 1920s and '30s was sometimes known as "froufrou" and they repeat the "less is more" mantra as the eleventh commandment. Yet there has, nonetheless, long been a compulsion to inject graphic complexity and even planned superfluity into certain kinds of design—particularly print design.

Ornament's comeback in the late 1990s is even more widespread today. Decorative patterning, an offshoot of the current ornamental trend, is largely born of street-culture excessiveness in various media—from textiles to clothing to web to print. Illustrated letterforms are among new decorative tendencies. Lettering in variegated forms—stitching, scrawling, scraping, carving, and more—have added a more profound ornamental overlay to design of the twenty-first century. During the early 2000s, well over a decade after the computer became the primary design tool, squiggly serpentine, floral ornamentation was resurrected with a vengeance. Rebellion against the blandness of template-driven, computer-generated design has been one motivation. Another is the fact that complex drafting, once difficult, is now much simpler with computer programs, spawning a new appreciation for ornament.

During the mid- to late 1990s, digital type foundries produced scores of novelty faces made from nontraditional type materials, including such naturalistic ones as twigs, flowers, leaves, stamens, and pistils. In some instances, the plant is a perfect foil for modernist austerity. Lettering made from branches and bark has a long history of usage as a sign system for rustic homes and campsites, as well as for graphically illustrated lettering. One of the most popular nineteenth-century novelty faces was Figgins's Rustic or Log Cabin, made from logs. Current usage is possibly more ironic, but not always. When done well it can be surrealistically beautiful and comically engaging, but when done poorly it is best as kindling.

What do I think of the current wave of squigglies? Deco-*flora* ornament is simply awful when misused. When well done, its exquisite, rhythmic complexity is pleasant to the eye. Yet this resurgence of floriated madness, which continues to engulf advertisements, magazine and book covers, textiles, T-shirts, package designs, and more, is becoming a nonsensical and overgrown design conceit, impossible to control. Maybe now's the time to prune. Or maybe just let it grow and see what happens.

---

Adapted from this article's original publication in *EYE* magazine, issue no. 72, Summer 2009.

## DISCUSSION POINTS

- Can graphic design history be divided according to unique styles and mannerisms?

- What is squiggly design reacting to or against?

- Is ornament or decoration a positive attribute in all graphic design?

- What does ornament or decoration add to design or typography?

*Every generation has a formative period. As a "Baby Bloomer," what I call the tail end of the "baby boom" of postwar children (now in their sixties and seventies), the mid- to late-1960s was a defining cultural, political, and social era. Years ago, when my memory was still at 90 percent of its capacity (don't ask what it is today), I wrote this recollection mixed with historical research and interviews on the design phenomena and language of this time. Despite being unfinished, it weighs in at more than 12,500 words. It is the longest essay in the book and maybe the most consequential.*

# Recalling the Sixties

## Introduction: Innocence, Maturity, Anarchy

After ingesting sufficient quantities of stimulants, Titus, a cartoonist with whom I had been pals during the late 1960s, often entertained his acquaintances with parodies of those late-night TV commercials for cut-rate nostalgic record albums. I remember this one as though it were yesterday:

> "Not available in any store at any price," he wailed in an irritating AM announcer's voice. "Farkas Records presents the greatest protest songs of the sixties. Civil Rights! Anti-war! Feminism! Gay Lib! Prison Uprising! Relive the march on Washington with your favorites by Phil Ochs, Joan Baez, Pete Seeger, Peter Paul and Mary, the Buffalo Springfield, and Country Joe and the Fish! On three records or two cassettes! And there's more: if you demonstrate now you'll get an extra television bonus: ten great consciousness-raisers by Bob 'The Times They Are A-Changin', Dylan! When do we want it? Now! So call (212) P-R-O-T-E-S-T today!"

Though his intake of hallucinogens made Titus somewhat extraterrestrial, none of us who enjoyed his stoned wit would have called him clairvoyant. Yet twenty years later his precognition is borne out by a similarly grating commercial for a disk of sixties tunes currently airing on TV. The truth is that many of us have secretly bought this record set, proving a strong allegiance to the Aquarian age. While nostalgia can be a sweet diversion, for some it can also be a rather bitter obsession. So say the members of the newly constituted Society for the Advancement of Time, whose motto is "We Will End the Sixties in Your Lifetime." They fervently believe that nothing is more revolting than revivals of sixties kitsch.

Such intolerance is why I approached the design review of this decade with trepidation. After all, what graphic images do the sixties conjure if not kitsch? Psychedelics—gaudy posters printed in Day-Glo colors illuminated by stroboscopic lights; ethereal Beardsleyesque drawings; Peter Max's nauseating kaleidoscopic visions of nirvana. This response is indeed knee-jerk, but nonetheless valid. Every era produces clichés, and in the absence of total recall they become the foundation on which memory is built.

My perception of the sixties is so profoundly shaped by the artistic reactions to the decade's social turmoil that it is difficult to accept that the design aesthetic emanating from the "youth culture" was an exception, not the rule. While a decade is a convenient measure of cultural accomplishment, it is also an arbitrary one. Events and their repercussions are never so neatly categorized. Therefore, it would be wrong to say that the sixties were exclusively an era of psychedelia, hippies, or yippies. In fact, such manifestations prevailed only during the latter half of the decade and faded away by the early 1970s. Perhaps it would be better to analyze design according to generations, but this too is imprecise. If we are to believe the design annuals published during the sixties, the "underground" generation did not exist at all.

Throughout the decade, juries for the Art Directors Club of New York, the Type Directors Club, and the Society of Illustrators virtually ignored anarchic underground art and design. With the exception of a few psychedelic record album covers, Milton Glaser's Duchamp-inspired Dylan poster, and some posters and a cover or two from *Evergreen Review*, the only "counterculture" representation was "over-ground" work that borrowed

# *After all, what graphic images do the sixties conjure if not kitsch?*

underground graphic conceits. Not until 1972 was a real underground paper selected for the AIGA Cover Show (incidentally, the underground was all but dead by 1973).

Surprising? Not really. The professional organizations were composed of an old guard and a few young Turks (mostly male, I might add), but not the underground amateurs who practiced "design" as a means of personal and collective expression. Perhaps the content of the underground papers and comix were too raw for the conservative juries. So many members of the Society of Illustrators worked for the government and armed services during the sixties that it wasn't until 1972 that SI mounted an anti-war exhibition (curated by Alan E. Cober and Lou Myers). More likely, though, underground artists couldn't afford the entry fees, or didn't even care about such trivial pursuits if they could. Design, after all, was not the issue—changing the world was. And though a few underground "layout" artists rejected the anarchic clutter and ultimately became professional, most remained uninterested in formal design or classical typography.

For a more accurate picture of sixties design, we look not to the raucous manifestations of the youth culture but to the professional annuals, magazines, and exhibition catalogs documenting the advertising, promotion, product, and periodical design of the mainstream. From these documents we learn that the real emblems of sixties design are not the nuclear disarmament sign or the Woodstock logo but the rejuvenated marks for Bell Telephone, the American Broadcasting Company, Chase Manhattan Bank, and Mobil Oil. The sixties, certainly the first half, marked the maturation of American graphic design.

*If graphic design is indeed a metaphor for the social condition, then the significant work of the late fifties and early sixties suggests equilibrium.*

## Growing Pains

The experiments that characterize sixties graphics actually began in the mid-fifties. Before the advent of mega-design firms, the advertising agencies, in-house design departments, and type shops were laboratories for adventuresome (yet decidedly professional) designers to test the limits of their materials and push their clients' expectations. The loosening of strict convention was encouraged, in part, by clients demanding more eye-catching advertising and promotion—and by the new graphic arts technologies, especially photocomposition, which saved time and money and ultimately offered greater creative license.

Optimism underlies this creativity. The postwar middle class luxuriated in relative peace. Corporations were not generally viewed as insatiable profit mongers nor environmental criminals. Rather, American business and industry—from box manufactures to oil companies—fostered technological advances, which encouraged market surpluses, which in turn stimulated national pride. A citizenry that had stoically endured wartime deprivations happily embraced the new bounty. Advertising, corporate, and magazine designers helped promote this to the world.

If graphic design is indeed a metaphor for the social condition, then the significant work of the late fifties and early sixties suggests equilibrium. The best magazines and advertising were sober, witty, and self-assured. Corporate identity was rational. The grid, as an organizing tool, underscored this new rationality. Ornamentation, which had symbolized bourgeois excess earlier in the century, was in many areas rejected for clear and intelligent concepts. As the objectified photograph took center stage, romantic and sentimental illustration became less appealing. The best aspects of the European Modern movement's dictum that form follow function were adopted. But this ideal was not indiscriminately used. America was not chaste like Switzerland nor regimented like Germany—rather, it was boisterous and passionate. And so were American designers.

"Instead of a consistent national style," Alvin Eisenman said in a speech before the 1959 Typography USA seminar sponsored by the Type Directors Club, "we seem to have a consistent national variety." Indeed, sixties design was an amalgam of diverse and contradictory approaches—of action and reaction.

## Schools of Thought and Deed

The influence of European émigrés (Herbert Bayer, László Moholy-Nagy, Ladislav Sutnar, György Kepes, Herbert Matter, Leo Lionni, Alexey Brodovitch, and Will Burtin) and the native American moderns who established themselves in the late 1930s and '40s (Paul Rand, Lester Beall, Bradbury Thompson, William Golden, Alvin Lustig, and Cipe Pineles), most of whom were active during the sixties, contributed directly and indirectly to three paramount American design methods during the sixties: rational (or modern), eclectic (or historical)—both having developed during the fifties—and anarchic (or underground). Two other aesthetics, traditional and sentimental, the former adhering to classical aspects of book and type design and the latter linked to premodern layout and illustration approaches, were eclipsed by the others.

Under each rubric, however, are disparate subsets, as well as individuals who are not conveniently pigeonholed. For example, under rational/ modern are the *strict formalists* representing the International school, including John Massey, Rudolph DeHarak, and Massimo Vignelli, who practiced objectified, systematic design. The *exuberant moderns*, such as Saul Bass, Lou Dorfsman, George Lois, Gene Federico, and Herb Lubalin, who were known for their ability to humanize design and make type speak. The *eclectic moderns* such as Robert Brownjohn, Ivan Chermayeff, Thomas Geismar, Tony Paladino, Jim Miho, and Bob Gill (who helped found London Pentagram in 1960), who routinely broke the rules and veered away from a single style. The *crypto moderns* such as the corporate identity firms of

Walter Landor and Lippincott and Margulies, who made generalized identity systems using ambient forms. And straddling the fence between eclectic and modern were the *magazine moderns* such as Henry Wolf, Alan Hurlburt, Peter Palazzo, Marvin Israel, Bea Feitler, and Ruth Ansel, who used rationally designed formats as a means to exuberantly present a wide variety of subjects.

Under the eclectic banner the subcategories run the gamut from historical revivalist to idiosyncratically playful. Push Pin Studios represents the most devoutly eclectic (and most profoundly influential), having revived the denigrated styles of Victorian, art nouveau, and art deco, and by having reintroduced narrative illustration to the design equation. Peter Max and Tom Daly (Daly & Max) and Phil Gips (Gips Danne) did likewise through their use of stylized illustration and rare wood types. Quite a few art directors and designers also fit into this general category, among them Bob Cato and John Berg, whose CBS record album cover design were archetypal; Harris Lewine, who had a liberal view of what made a good book jacket and so hired both eclectics and moderns to design them; Neil Fujita and Robert Scudelari, who did book jackets that knew no stylistic constraints; Otto Storch, whose format for *McCall's* was alternately the paradigm of the new ornamentation and a paean to functionalism; Art Paul, whose approach to *Playboy* magazine was a departure from gridlock; Arnold Varga, whose advertisements for Joseph Horne Co. updated old forms, including decoupage; and Ed Benguiat, who brought a nineteenth-century spirit to twentieth-century typography.

To further confuse matters of categorization, some of the modern pioneers became eclectic when it suited them. Despite Herbert Bayer's execration of Victorian ornamental typefaces in advertising as "bad taste under the disguise of functionalism par excellence," he designed posters for Aspen, Colorado, using ornamental typography combined with modernistic collage. Bradbury Thompson routinely used nineteenth-century engravings from Diderot as a foil for his modern typography. And Herb Lubalin, the master of talking type, also did his share of Victorian layouts—when, of course, the subject called for it.

Patterns resulting in these sixties aesthetics developed along generational lines. Many of the graphic designers who began working before World War II were Depression-era kids from immigrant or otherwise poor families,

*As the root of postwar American design, European modernism attracted those interested in more than just mechanical commercial art.*

exposed to commercial art in high school as an alternative to more mundane labor. By introducing his students to the great European graphic designers, Leon Friend, the head of the graphics department at Brooklyn's Abraham Lincoln High School beginning in the late 1930s, taught them to be creative, not just do routine agency work. Modern design symbolized a break from their parents' old-world ties. And for those who pursued the field after high school, pioneer instructors such as Howard Trafton at the Art Students League and Herschel Levitt and Tom Benrimo at Pratt Institute in New York opened more doors to the expressive realms of graphic design.

For the generation that graduated high school after the war, other leading schools with European faculty members offered more advanced courses of study, including Yale University in New Haven, MIT in Cambridge, and the Art Institute in Chicago, which proffered the neo-Bauhausian approach. The Chouinard Art Institute in Los Angeles and the School of Visual Arts in New York were spawning grounds for eclectics, and Cooper Union in New York graduated some of the decade's leading moderns and eclectics. These same schools also graduated some members of the "third" generation.

For members of the first two generations, graphic design was a dialectic—the proponents of modern versus advocates of variegated form. As the root of postwar American design, European modernism attracted those interested in more than just mechanical commercial art. As a teenager in the 1930s, Paul Rand was introduced to the Bauhaus and speaks for many of his contemporaries about its influence: "I was intrigued with that kind of work which focused on ideas and not banalities; which stressed painting, architecture, typography and showed how they interrelated."

Rand and others fought for radical notions of commercial art within the business fraternity, thereby snatching design out of the print shop and forging a real profession.

Belief in the rightness of form was key to this revolution, but not at the expense of wit and humor. Some practiced economy, promoted the virtues of white space, and imbued their work with measured expression. Others rejected expression entirely, favoring a systematic Swiss method of visual organization being successfully applied to corporate communications and product and exhibition design where order was imperative. But as for more ephemeral posters and record and book jackets . . . well, here is where the revolt begins.

Jan Tschichold, author of *The New Typography* in 1928, wrote in 1959 that "a certain Swiss approach of today . . . for which I do not feel responsible, is the exemplar of a most inflexible typography which makes no distinction between the advertising of an artistic performance or of a screw catalog. Nor does this typography allow for the human desire for variety. It has an entirely militaristic attitude." Some designers entering the profession in the 1950s agreed that Swiss purity ran counter to the requisite that design of these more "playful" media be jovial.

The Push Pin style was the most visible example of design pluralism. It began as a visceral response to Seymour Chwast, Reynold Ruffins, and Ed Sorel's urban influences, notably the comics. Yet according to Milton Glaser, who also helped found Push Pin Studios in 1955, it was a reaction to absolutism in design: "We frequently find corruption more interesting than purity," he says. "Much that is ideologically sound is also thoroughly uninteresting . . . ideological things rob people and objects of their energy." Owing to Push Pin's skill at self-promotion, their eclectic revivals, and most importantly their unique inventions, were warmly accepted by publishing and entertainment industry clients. Like-minded designers who objected to rigidity also turned to the "big closet" of historical precedents for inspiration. While some used these artifacts as a springboard to achieve unprecedented work, others flagrantly stole fully realized ideas. Underscoring an increased need for source material, the Bettmann Archive in New York, that incalculable storehouse of printed ephemera, did whopping business during those years. And in 1963, Otto Bettmann and Peter Max were co-curators of *Bettmann*

*Panoptican*, an exhibition designed to show how the archive contributed to the range of what was then dubbed the "New Romantic" style.

The downside of the New Romanticism was eclectic folly as ornamentally excessive as the theoretical approach was sterile. The basic problem with both extremes was described by Paul Rand in "Modern Typography in the Modern World," an astute article that originally appeared in 1952 in the British journal *Typographica 5*: "We have inherited from the great esthetic revolution of the twentieth century the task of bringing to fruition the new ideas and forms which it introduced. This task is not only arduous but less rewardingly glamorous than was participation in the original dramatic and dynamic insurgence. Consequently, many designers and typographers have shirked this task. Some have contracted the revolutionary habit of novelty making—neglecting other aspects of design and indulging in a sort of perpetual juvenilism. Other designers, unable to escape the academic habit, have to soon crystalized the theories of the esthetic revolution into a set of rules and dogma."

Actually, by the sixties, strict modern canons were anachronistic—vestiges of the social and moral issues of a bygone age. Even those designers most sympathetic to the Bauhaus were charting their own courses. John Massey, director of communications for the Container Corporation of America for twenty-six years, said of his influences, "I have always believed that the Bauhaus tradition had in its breadth enough facets and opportunities to include a great variety of images and approaches." The firm of Brownjohn, Chermayeff & Geismar opened their New York office in 1957 and soon epitomized an American Late Modern diversity. "We were uninterested in nostalgia," says Tom Geismar, "but were not reluctant to use it when appropriate. In fact, often on Saturdays we would go to Coney Island to photograph signs and buildings for use in our work." And many savvy young designers did what Henry Wolf, then art director of *Show* magazine, confessed to doing in a speech before the 1962 Eyes West design conference in San Francisco: "You swipe from many sources and the combination of the sources evolves a style for yourself. Paul Rand swiped from Paul Klee and I swipe from Paul Rand and yet Rand doesn't look like Klee and I hope, sometimes, I don't look like Rand, because I also swipe from others."

# The Birth of an American Style

The most provocative confluence of modern and eclectic ideas occurred in the advertising of the fifties and early sixties. Advertising was in a state of war, with two rival factions battling for supremacy. On one side were the veteran agency journeymen who, as slaves to copywriters, made uninspired use of type and image; on the other, a coterie of younger "designers" who used bold, economical forms to elevate the level of communication. Taking a cue from editorial, print advertising became more conceptually acute. Ideas replaced cliched slogans, and thought-provoking imagery supplanted boring product shots or puerile cartoons. Though the new eventually won, the old still lingers.

Many of the art director/designers participating in the sixties print advertising revolution contributed to the fifties hothouse mentality. Helmut Krone's ad for the New Haven Railroad (1955), titled "The Clearest Road into New York," prefigured his breakthrough Volkswagen ads; given its witty concept, Krone's railway ad did, in a simple picture and clever slogan, what similar ads took paragraphs to say. Hershel Bramson's ads for Smirnoff vodka (1956), with exquisite photography by Bert Stern, were among the first ads to show a product eclipsed by an abstract and moody image. Continuing the creative tradition started by Paul Rand in the 1940s, Robert Gage's campaign for Orbach's (1957) wed action, rather than stiff, fashion photography, to expressive typography. Saul Bass's dramatic newspaper ad for *Champion* (1949), a totally black page with a tiny halftone and small handwritten scrawl in the center, prefigured his later metaphorical movie posters and logos. Applying an editorial sensibility to CBS radio and television ads, Louis Dorfsman proved that "smart message" advertising highlighted by expressive typography could have a profound impact. Likewise, Louis Silverstein's ads for the *New York Times* expertly employed the "candid" journalistic photograph, and Herbert Matter's photomontages for Knoll's advertising showed how far abstraction could be pushed in the service of commerce. By the beginning of the sixties, these "experiments" in advertising form and content had proven successful.

The struggle between advertising and editorial departments for reader/viewer attention continues, but in the early sixties the tide began to turn in favor of advertising. Evidence provided in the Art Directors Club annuals suggests that while many noteworthy periodicals were published during this period, advertising was no longer visually or conceptually subservient to magazine content. Indeed, for the better part of the decade, advertising was such an influential design medium that for many of the editorial art directors interviewed for this article, it was the model.

## Advertising: Less Is the Key

The sixties were the golden age of print advertising because creative teams of art directors and copywriters worked, more or less, in harmony. Television had not yet seduced these talented partners away. Art directors—the best art directors—were also graphic designers. They understood the nuances of type and made ideas come alive through its intelligent handling. The canard that advertising had to talk down to the consumer was rejected with one simple word: Lemon.

"In the beginning, there was Volkswagen," wrote Jerry Della Femina in his 1970 bestselling memoir of the ad business, *From Those Wonderful Folks Who Gave You Pearl Harbor*. That's the first campaign that everyone can trace back and say, "This is where the changeover began." The changeover was the 1959 Volkswagen "Think Small" campaign, art directed by Helmut Krone for Doyle Dane Bernbach. In an era when advertising accentuated mythic perfection, this was the first time that an advertiser admitted to the possibility of imperfection. Not only that, but given the Promethean car mentality, the Volkswagen was already an underdog. The copy said that once in a while VW turns out a lemon, and if they do they get rid of it. "No one had ever called his product a lemon before," continues Della Femina. "It was the first time anyone really took a realistic approach to advertising. It was the first time the advertiser ever talked to the consumer as though he was a grownup instead of a baby."

The campaign was also so visually distinctive that it became the quintessential American ad. Krone allowed ample white space to frame a modest Futura Bold headline, and the matter-of-fact photography dispelled the idea that automobile photography should be high gloss. It was also the first time that advertising copy was allowed to be conversational and have

## Advertising was a somewhat genteel profession until the street-smart sons and daughters of immigrants broke into the ranks.

widows to avoid artificially filling out lines. Perhaps anticipating some residual ill feeling from World War II, the VW logo was kept small.

Virtually everything Doyle Dane Bernbach touched turned to gold. Another momentous campaign was for Levy's Rye Bread, art directed by William Taubman. Though the difference in the taste of rye breads is negligible, the sudden rash of posters showing either an African American or Chinese child and an Indian or Chinese man happily munching on a sandwich under the headline "You Don't Have to Be Jewish to Love Levy's" is as memorable today as Doyle Dane's classic sixties "We Try Harder" campaign for Avis.

During the forties and fifties, endearing trade characters were ubiquitous. By the sixties, many of these pixies and gnomes were replaced by more sophisticated concepts. About one famous change, Della Femina recalls that "They were trying to sell Alka-Seltzer with this little Speedy creep. Well one day they moved the account over to Jack Tinker and the first thing Tinker did was to kill off Speedy, or if they didn't kill him they had him arrested in the men's room of Grand Central Station. . . . And they came up with a great campaign, 'Alka Seltzer on the Rocks.'" To make a chalky-tasting medicine into a refreshing cocktail was a stroke of brilliance. This was the age of smart ideas *and* great execution.

Advertising was a somewhat genteel profession until the street-smart sons and daughters of immigrants broke into the ranks. George Lois, whose agency Papert Koenig Lois churned out many gems, was one of these brash, tough-talking wunderkinds. He was also a remarkable art director who would conceive a great idea, sell it to a client through force of will, and then make it typographically sing. He did this with the campaign for Wolfschmidt vodka, in which the bottle of the tasteless liquor is seen chatting with some tasty additives, such as a lime and tomato. Not all his campaigns were successful, but all had a certain irreverence that made advertising relate more to the human experience.

The sixties were *the* decade of public service (*pro bono public*) advertising. Since the advertising business communicated directly to the American mainstream, it accomplished more than the counterculture to raise white middle-class consciousness to the problems of those Americans being discriminated against in housing, education, and the workplace. Harnessing commercial advertising techniques, Young and Rubicam's "Give a Damn" campaign for the Urban Coalition exemplified the new confrontational public service message. It was bold yet did not scare its audience off. It also conditioned viewers to relate to public service ads with even more startling imagery, such as Doyle Dane Bernbach's rat control ad, art directed by Burt Steinhauser, which shows a life-size rat with the headline "Cut this out and put it in bed next to your child." So effectively did it castigate congressmen who voted against a bill to provide rat control in slum areas that when the bill finally passed, Steinhauser received a letter from President Johnson that said "your . . . advertising must surely have played an important part in persuading the Congress of the necessity for this vital legislation." Advertising was indeed flexing its muscles.

## Television and Its Impact on Typography

With the new advertising came, quite literally, new vehicles. The sides and tops of buses became moving billboards, viewed as one would view the fleeting images on a television screen. As the pace of life changed, the pace of turning magazine pages also quickened in direct proportion to the popularity of TV. This forced typographers to compete with the television medium, consciously or not.

Herb Lubalin was not satisfied that type communicated its message clearly. He was compelled to present both the message and the pictorial idea in one image. "Television has had its effect," he wrote as early as 1960. "We are becoming more accustomed to looking at pictures and less in reading lengthy copy. The resulting trend in advertising has been toward large pictorial elements and short, sparkling headline copy. . . . These influences have created a need for experimentation. . . . One of the important results is . . . the typographic image." As practiced by Lubalin, the "word picture" challenged the inertia of traditional typography by eliminating leading between lines, removing letterspacing, and altering type forms. In keeping with the TV aesthetic, Lubalin contended that the designer "has resorted to distortion and disfiguration of type forms, but the obvious emotional result often lends justification to these disfigurations."

"Today, the predominance of images over text is a clear indication of a gradual transition from an intellectual to a sensory civilization," wrote Aldo Novarese, the designer of the typeface Micrograma, in an article explaining his design of his other sans serif, Eurostile. "This new typeface should be considered a symbol of our present civilization exactly as other faces represented and were the expression of other civilizations in the past." Indeed, Eurostile—which some critics argued tried so hard to be modern that it became a novelty face—based its form on icons of the era, particularly its "o," which resembles the typical shape of television screens of the time.

## McLuhan's Predictions

The influence of television on the print medium also prompted philosophical enquiry into the future of print itself. Marshall McLuhan was perhaps the most controversial savant of the decade, and in 1964 he predicted the demise of print in the age of telecommunications. McLuhan argued that the invention of print changed society from a collective with oral traditions, with memory as the supreme storehouse of information, to a cult of individualism. This happened because information could be put down on paper by a lone person in a solitary environment. McLuhan asserted that it did not matter whether books were read or not, because just the physical act of transcription and printing gave rise to categorization, specialization, and ultimately alienation. Print shattered tribal unity into many splintered worlds, but with television tribal patterns would soon return. The television image was chaotic, not orderly; it demanded that people participate in the storytelling process. Forcing people back together through shared images would result in a new world community that McLuhan called the Global Village.

*McLuhan asserted that it did not matter whether books were read or not, because just the physical act of transcription and printing gave rise to categorization, specialization, and ultimately alienation.*

## The Kinetic Book

Book design was the last bastion of historicists in their fight against modernity. During the sixties, however, the book entered the twentieth century with a vengeance. Quentin Fiore's design for McLuhan's *The Medium Is the Massage* and *War and Peace in the Global Village* (and later Jerry Rubin's *Do It!*) set the standard. Static page layout was eschewed for the kinetic experience. Fiore used sans serif body text of various weights and sizes to emphasize or highlight specific points. Black-and-white photographs were used, not as illustrations to underscore a text, but as information as inextricably tied to the content as any words. In the manner of a television transmission (and echoing McLuhan's argument), fragmented illustration throughout the book would periodically come together to form completed pictures. Fiore's approach was a link between the moving and static image that opened the door to more progressive experiments.

But before print (or, for that matter, paper) could be entirely replaced by electronics, a universal typographic language had to be developed. Despite serious attempts beginning in the 1920s to standardize letterforms, signs, and symbols, such regimentation has often met with resistance.

## Typography: Expression and Systemization

The International Style developed its typographic voice with the introduction of two sans serifs designed in the 1950s, Univers (by Adrian Frutiger) and Helvetica (by Eduard Hoffmann and Max Miedinger). Both were neutral, purposefully devoid of personality so as to eschew any interpretative components. As one critic described Helvetica, "it offers no ambiguity—the message is the message." Although successfully marketed in Europe, these faces were not immediately available in the United States because type was still primarily metal and required an enormous investment for fonts of various weights and sizes. Moreover, the modernists seemed content to use what was already available: Akidenz Grotesque, Trade Gothic, Lightline Gothic, and other sans serifs. However, when Mergenthaler introduced Helvetica in 1962, it became such a popular face that for a while it seemed to be the only type on the market. Even so, Helvetica and Univers never totally dominated American typographic taste. Designers during the sixties, like those of previous decades, were still interested in both the classics and the novelties.

"There are countries such as the United States," wrote Aaron Burns, guest editor of *Print*'s 1963 special issue on typography, "where typographic design radiates in all directions and in all fields, where competition between typographers and designers goes on daily, where national restrictions are few if any." As director of the Composing Room and later the principal of his own type business, Burns was a leader in the discipline known as "typographic design." Indeed, his oversized book *Typography* (1961) was an inspiring cogitation on the untapped expressive potential of hot metal typography as applied to the New Advertising, illustrated by a wealth of creative, rule-breaking applications. Burns was also a pioneer of photocomposition and literally dragged designers with whom he worked into the twentieth century by proving its utility. Toward this aim, he published a series of primers on the operation and application of this new technology. Though major suppliers Photo Lettering Inc., Varitype, Compugraphics, and Visual Graphics Corporation fervently promoted the new technology, Burns made the most convincing argument for its widespread use, breaking down the considerable resistance to photocomposition among art and type directors.

Yet even during the sixties there were significant holdouts. Tom Geismar admits that since he preferred the "kiss" of hot metal, Chermayeff & Geismar did not switch to cold type until hot type was no longer economically viable—or available. Conversely, to accomplish his typographic pyrotechnics, Herb Lubalin immediately and zealously embraced the new form, carving out a niche as the "master" of phototype design. With Lubalin's work as the model, many young designers began to specify phototype set excruciatingly tight in the manner known as "smashed" typography. Burns once confided that he thought Lubalin, his one-time partner and close friend, went a little too far. What Lubalin had intended as expression too quickly became a misused conceit.

On the revival front, Morgan and Morgan published specimen books of Victorian wood types. Some critics argued that this trivialized typographic design, while others savored these faces for their romantic character. Working with Herb Lubalin, Tom Carnese customized many historically derived letterforms, and Tony DeSpigna revived calligraphy as a viable method. Toward the end of the decade, hundreds of old metal and wood typefaces had been transferred to film, and Photo Lettering Inc. offered a panoply of redrawn and reinterpreted Victorian, art nouveau, and art deco display faces.

## Magazines: Storehouses of Inspiration

While modern typography supplanted hand lettering in advertising, eclectic typography enlivened the traditional magazine spread. *McCall's* art director Otto Storch was one of the preeminent revivalists, yet his layouts never looked nostalgic. The trick of reviving things was not to mimic the past, but to give it new life. Storch was not, however, content to prolong his "trendsetting" formula for long. In 1965 at an AIGA conference called Magazine: U.S.A., Storch announced his intention of initiating a new format. "Some of the things I've done in the past," he admitted, "I think now are a little over-designed. I'm beginning to feel that a simpler, quieter approach is better." Indeed, Storch was speaking for many art directors when he announced: "a magazine doesn't have to be a circus where you keep jumping through a hoop with each spread."

*Monocle* was one magazine published during the early sixties where the circus reference is apt. Edited by Victor Navasky and art directed by Phil Gips, this oblong-shaped magazine was stridently satiric, prefiguring *National Lampoon* and *Spy*. The magazine even ran one of its contributing editors, Marvin Kitman, for president to disrupt the Republican party ticket. *Monocle* was three times a proving ground. First, its Victorian-inspired design, with pages that often resembled nineteenth-century circus posters, helped popularize a "retro" approach. Second, it relied exclusively on illustration for pictorial needs, so Gips assembled the best commercial illustrators around—who also turned out to be some of wittiest graphic commentators of the decade, including Seymour Chwast, Edward Sorel, Milton Glaser, Tomi Ungerer, Lou Myers, David Levine, R. O. Blechman, Robert Grossman, Marshall Arisman, Randall Enos, Paul Davis, and John Alcorn. Lastly, it was the one of the few magazines since the *New Yorker* to publish sophisticated social and political humor. Though short-lived, it became a veritable clip file for some underground designers later in the decade.

The year before John F. Kennedy was assassinated, the rumblings of social conflict were becoming audible in Berkeley and elsewhere. The early sixties thus began a fertile period of political/cultural publishing. Rooted in the limited circulation "literary magazine" sensibility, the New York–based *The Second Coming*, art directed by Tony Paladino, and the San Francisco–based *Contact*, art directed by Nicholas Sidjakov and Jerry Richardson, became archetypes of the New Left counterculture journal. Owing to limited means, type was confined to transfer letters or whatever the printer had in his type case. The layouts were nevertheless clean and curiously irreverent, and provided signposts for future design directions.

*Evergreen Review* was the next evolutionary stage. It began as a quarto-sized Beat journal featuring fiction, poetry, and drama. In the mid-sixties under editor Barney Rosset and art director Richard Hess, it increased in size and expanded its content to become a full-fledged magazine with color covers, erotic portfolios, political commentary, and ribald comic strips. Like *Monocle*, *Evergreen* used Push Pin members and kindred illustrators to position itself as alternative culture. Later, under the precise art direction of Kenneth Deardorf, *Evergreen* became a primary outlet for the next generation of illustrators.

In 1964, Warren Hinckle, Robert Scheer (an activist editor), and Dugald Stermer (an equally activist graphic designer) transformed *Ramparts*, a failing two-year-old San Francisco–based radical Catholic magazine, into an investigative national monthly. Its restrained, albeit flexible, format was based on classic book design; its signature was the Oxford rule and Times Roman typeface. "Our design had to be credible," says Stermer, "because we were saying incredible things." Stories on women's and gay rights, political folly, and covert government intrigue were regular ingredients. For *Ramparts'* graphic commentary, Stermer used Carl Fischer's strident montages and startlingly staged pictures (one, showing four hands holding burning draft cards, caused a Washington inquiry). Stermer also developed a visual identity around artists like Gene Holtan, Ben Shahn, and Push Pin alumni. When *Ramparts* published "University on the Make," an article that exposed Michigan State University for willingly providing cover to CIA operations in South Vietnam, much of the fuss and fury aroused was due to Paul Davis's malicious cover painting of Madame Nhu in a cheerleader's pose, wielding the MSU banner. Edward Sorel further irritated the powers with his "Sorel's Bestiary," a monthly graphic commentary that explored the similarities between leading cultural/political bêtes noirs and their animal relations. Sam Antupit credited Stermer's work as the model for the design of some late-sixties periodicals.

If the measure of a successful magazine is how it reflects the time in which it publishes, then *Esquire* and *Playboy* are among the sixties' most sacred documents. Each not only reported on events and issues, they helped to make them. During the fifties, *Esquire* had been the quintessence of urbanity, having evolved from a men's magazine into a bible of contemporary culture and mores. Art directed for twelve years by Henry Wolf, *Esquire*'s persona defined an American bon ton—a rather rarefied approach to life that was eventually eclipsed by sixties turmoil. After leaving the magazine to replace Alexey Brodovitch as art director of *Harper's Bazaar*, Wolf was briefly replaced by Robert Benton, who was eventually followed by Sam Antupit (Wolf's former associate at *Bazaar*). Owing to Antupit's graphic wit

*If the measure of a successful magazine is how it reflects the time in which it publishes, then* Esquire *and* Playboy *are among the sixties' most sacred documents.*

and his editor Harold Hayes's social concern, each issue of *Esquire* had its finger on the pulse of the liberal body politic. Though a monthly, *Esquire*'s stories were pegged to those issues uppermost in its readers' minds, and its acerbic parodies (most notably the "Dubious Achievement Awards") were consistently on target. Even its fashion features had a certain raw edge.

Using relatively quiet typography and not overdesigning every spread, Antupit allowed conceptual art and photography to bear the editorial weight. That *Esquire* was a magazine of ideas, not decorative trivialities, was further underscored by George Lois's poster-like concepts for covers that were photographically rendered by Carl Fischer. For over two years, Lois worked directly with Hayes on covers that made trenchant graphic commentaries rather than advertising the contents of the magazine. Fischer's ironic photographic manipulations of Andy Warhol being sucked into a can of soup, Richard Nixon being made up to appear more presidential, and a frighteningly banal portrait of Lt. William Calley (My Lai) posing with a group of Asian children are cultural icons as anthropologically revealing as any ancient artifact. Moreover, they underscore the power of the static image over TV. Despite the satiric breakthroughs of such humorous sixties TV series as *That Was the Week That Was*, television executives were loath to risk libel and slander suits or offending the undefined mass audience with hard-hitting commentaries.

*Esquire* appeared to be fearless, yet it was usually found in doctors' waiting rooms, suggesting that it was not really a threat to the status quo. On the other hand, even during the libertine sixties, *Playboy* was reserved for home reading. Hugh Hefner was not only a former employee but a devout fan of *Esquire*, and his new magazine, originally titled *Stag Party* but changed to *Playboy* when it premiered in 1953, was the next evolutionary step in men's magazines. The key was its unholy union of erotic photography with serious fiction and nonfiction, designed in such a handsome package as to not look the least bit tawdry. The first few issues designed by a young illustrator, Art Paul, who continued as its art director for twenty-eight years, were done with limited resources. "I used the type that the printer had available," recalled Paul, "and chose Baskerville and Stymie because they were masculine typefaces." By the early sixties *Playboy* was not just a magazine—it embodied a philosophy that was as politically in tune with the age as was possible before the raising of women's consciousness. Though its content seems schizophrenic, the mix of sex, journalism, and literature was in fact decidedly progressive. Moreover, its design represented advanced visual thinking, especially in the field of illustration.

"I tried to be adventurous to a fault," said Paul. He provided mural-like spaces for paintings and drawings and sought out painters whose work lent itself to illustrative use (among them Ed Paschke, Tom Wesselman, and members of the Chicago group known as the Hairy Who) in addition to those "young illustrators trying to discover themselves." The key to a successful *Playboy* illustration, said Paul, "is finding the essence rather than the literal idea. From the outset I was not interested in drawings which required captions." Paul believed illustration was a cooperative effort, and even convinced certain authors to write to the art. In *Playboy*, collaboration was also evident in the various paper "tricks" (die cuts, inserts, and fold overs) that Paul called "participatory graphics," included in every issue. By the end of the sixties, *Playboy* had developed a genre of realistic and impressionistic illustration and had launched the careers of many artists who would lead the field in the seventies.

As the sexual revolutionaries mounted the barricades in 1962, Ralph Ginzburg, another *Esquire* alumnus, founded *Eros*, a sumptuously produced hardcover review of eroticism. Its content was not prurient, but rather an amalgam of sex in art and literature with provocative portfolios. The most taboo-smashing was titled "Black and White in Color," a "photographic poem by Ralph M. Hattersley Jr." with introductory copy that read: "Interracial couples of today bear the indignity of having to defend their love to a questioning world. Tomorrow these couples will be recognized as pioneers of an enlightened age. . . ." For the job of *Eros*'s art director/designer, Ginzburg (who was eventually jailed for using the United States mails—postmarked from Intercourse, Pennsylvania—to sell the "contraband" magazine) selected Herb Lubalin. From the very first issue, Lubalin's expressive advertising typography was brilliantly applied to magazine layout. *Eros* had an advantage over the weekly and monthly magazines because it had no advertising to fight with editorial. But such a competitive edge should not disqualify Lubalin's design as being a milestone, nor should it exempt Lubalin from being one of the decade's leading magazine art directors.

*Fact* was another productive collaboration for Ginzburg and Lubalin. With its premiere issue in 1964, *Fact* positioned itself as a New Left alternative to the liberal *New Republic* and the anti-left *New Leader* (which Lubalin also later designed). It was designed for easy reading, with wide columns of large Times Roman text usually illuminated by full-page conceptual illustrations (by artists such as Ettienne Delesert and Chas. B. Slackman) facing each story. Often one illustrator would do the entire issue. Design was of primary importance, and in the first issue Ginzburg announced that *Fact* would be "a handsome magazine, elegantly art-directed." About the art direction, Lubalin noted in an interview: "I had to come up with a format that would be so rigid that the cost of designing each issue would be kept to a minimum. Everything had to be figured out beforehand down to the last character of type. . . . From that point on, I didn't have to 'design' the books at all. All I had to do was select the illustrator. . . ." Each cover was a typographic billboard that sold the lead story by using the ambient advertising technique. One such was the issue with the inflammatory statement: "Fact: 1,189 Psychiatrists Say Goldwater Is Psychologically Unfit To Be President!" over which Goldwater sued for libel and won.

In 1961, Lubalin was asked by the *Saturday Evening Post*'s art director Ken Stewart to design some feature stories in an effort to, as Frank Zachary wrote, "replace a rather dowdy Midwestern image with a more contemporary look." Circulation was sliding and the business department thought that sprucing up the *Post*'s look would have beneficial results. But the patient was near death and cosmetics were not going to help. More importantly, says Stewart, "Lubalin really didn't understand our readership. They weren't interested in his brilliant typographic styling, they wanted Norman Rockwell and felt safe with very literal art." Though Lubalin was not well suited this very conservative publication, he was the perfect choice to art direct *Avant Garde*. As the title suggests, this was perhaps one of the most progressive-looking publications of the age. It was square, like a record jacket, giving the magazine an immediate distinction and allowing Lubalin great flexibility with layout. *Avant Garde* was Ginzburg's opportunity to unite the contents of *Eros* and *Fact* into one journal, and Lubalin used every thematic opportunity to make riveting typographical images. But his most enduring invention was the angular *Avant Garde* logo with its decidedly modern ligatures. Avant Garde, the typeface, was subsequently marketed and became a frequently misused alternative to Futura and Helvetica.

Some magazines are "of their time," and others are "for their time." *Rolling Stone* represents the latter and *Eye* the former. *Rolling Stone* was originally a tabloid designed by John Williams, who copied, rule for rule, the format of *The Daily Ramparts* (a San Francisco strike paper designed by Dugald Stermer, for whom Williams worked as an assistant). The cover, however, was slightly different; it was quarter-folded using separate paper stock and had a hand-drawn logo by San Francisco comix artist Rick Griffin. Sometime during the first year, Robert Kingsbury was hired as the new art director. Kingsbury was publisher Jann Wenner's brother-in-law and, more importantly, a painter who knew little about conventional magazine design, but nevertheless developed a strong visual persona using some old tabloid tricks (e.g. silhouetted photographs, spot color, and duo-tones). Before *Rolling Stone*, there were two extremes of music journalism—the adolescent teeny-bop magazines (*Sixteen* and *Tiger Beat*) and the industry newspapers (*Billboard*). *Rolling Stone* elevated the discourse by fusing stories about the industry, personality features, and music news with writing informed by the politics of the day. *Rolling Stone* got better and better from year to year, and vast improvements in visual and editorial content could be seen from issue to issue. Even in its early years it set a design standard for alternate culture journals (as it was ostensibly the first professionally designed underground paper). It was also the first national publication that defiant youth could really call their own.

In the late fifties there were large-circulation magazines for teenage girls, like *Seventeen* (art directed by Art Kane) and *Junior Bazaar* (art directed by Bob Cato). But the sixties marked a profound increase in baby boomer buying power. Fashions and entertainments aimed at youth dominated the marketplace, and in 1968 the Hearst Company decided to cash in. *Eye* was their attempt to harness youth culture and to lure record company, cosmetic, and other lifestyle advertising away from more traditional media. "*Eye* was doomed to failure," says Sam Antupit, who designed the original format. "It was conceived by the parents of the kids they were hoping to attract to teach lessons that the kids weren't interested in." Hearst wanted to market a good magazine and so gave it tremendous support (*Eye* even had discrete offices in Greenwich Village, many blocks from Hearst headquarters). But even these supportive executives had no idea what they were getting into. After all, this was the era of sex, drugs, and rock and roll, and *Eye* was not was not committed to the ethic. *Eye* was a preppie in hippie clothing. Its look was defined by psychedelicized deco typefaces, rainbow-colored borders, and photographs of the latest Carnaby Street fashions, but ultimately it tried too hard to be "of the times" and so lacked the conviction of both the more conventional magazines it hoped to surpass and the underground papers it could never emulate.

As fashion magazines go, only one was genuinely vanguard. In 1964, two former assistants of *Harper's Bazaar*'s art director Marvin Israel, Bea Feitler and Ruth Ansel, took charge as co-art directors. Two decades earlier, Alexey Brodovitch had eliminated the static fashion photograph, and Feitler and Ansel saw "the visual idiom of the magazine as more and more cinematic, a photographic means of grasping the elusive 'now' of fashion," wrote a critic in 1967. Drawing inspiration from pop art and underground cinema, *Harper's Bazaar* dramatically represented the glitter side of the "expanding visual experience" of the sixties.

Two other "for their times" magazines published on opposite coasts. *West*, the Sunday supplement of the *Los Angeles Times*, was exceptionally art directed by former *Playboy* designer Mike Salisbury, who was eclectic

*Some magazines are "of their time," and others are "for their time."* Rolling Stone *represents the latter and* Eye *the former.*

to a fault. If Frank Zachary is correct and "art direction is the handmaiden of the editorial idea and not its mistress," then one might accuse Salisbury of pulverizing accepted mores. More accurately, though, he invested this originally "male oriented" supplement with a cacophony of visual treats that transcended its original editorial intent. Salisbury's design was content—and it was the liveliest presentation of visual stimuli of the decade.

In New York, Milton Glaser entered a partnership with editor Clay Felker (another *Esquire* alumnus) that resulted in the 1968 revival of *New York,* the former supplement of the defunct *Herald Tribune,* as a weekly magazine devoted to contemporary city life. A virtual novice to the field of magazine design, Glaser developed a subdued format that relied on illustration and photography for graphic impact. Though the first issue's contributors included Tom Wolfe, Jimmy Breslin, Gloria Steinem, and Clare Booth Luce, *New York* was basically unfocused. It also failed to attract sizable readership. But when former *Esquire* associate art director Walter Bernard was hired as the art director (Glaser took an active conceptual role with the title Design Director), the layout got tighter and was primed for surprise. Moreover, the quirky coverage of the city, which became *New York*'s trademark, began to coalesce. Because the art budget was meager, the covers of the early issues were generic cityscapes. However, Bernard managed to persuade Carl Fischer to do his conceptual wizardry and become a frequent contributor. And since *New York* was, not coincidentally, headquartered in the same brownstone as Push Pin Studios, Bernard availed himself of their talents as well. Seymour Chwast did poster covers for special "seasonal" issues, and Sorel, Grossman, Davis, and Barbara Nessim contributed too. Spot art was

*Conceptual illustration, which has often been credited as the invention of the* New York Times *op-ed page, was perfected five years earlier in the news and feature sections of the* Sunday Trib.

used to maximum efficiency; one illustrator, such as Chas. B. Slackman or Jan Faust, would regularly illustrate a back- or front-of-the-book column. *New York* (which has been publishing for over fifty years now) had covered the city throughout the seventies with wit and irreverence, as well as the concern and conscience borne of the sixties.

## Newspapers: The Final Frontier

When *New York* premiered in 1963, it was the Sunday magazine supplement of the *New York Herald Tribune*. It was also the flagship of a redesigned fleet of Sunday news sections commanded by design director Peter Palazzo. Although the title "art director" was not new to newspapers (the term is used in an 1897 *Tribune* type book), the *Trib* was the first contemporary newspaper to hire a full-time design director to implement radical changes in a medium that had been only slightly tampered with in over fifty years. *The Trib* was one of twelve New York City dailies fiercely competing for newsstand sales and reader loyalty. Though the daily *Trib* basically held its own against its leading competitor, the *New York Times*, on Sunday the latter consistently blew the former out of the water. *The Trib*'s owner, John Hay Whitney, believed that extreme measures were required to make any noticeable impact on sales. Enter Palazzo, who said about the project in 1964: "An editorial as well as a design concept was needed because the design itself couldn't be changed without also changing . . . the traditional approach to the news." This meant "more careful editorial planning and editing of stories in a feature magazine way." With a commitment from the editors to make unprecedented adjustments (and prefiguring current computerized newspaper makeup), Palazzo designed a modular format, which acted as an automatic organizer for many news items on the page. He selected Caslon as the principal typeface because "of the instant impression of integrity it gives to the news." White space, always considered a taboo in newspaper makeup, was key to the new format.

Perhaps more remarkably, Palazzo (and his autonomous section designers, including Richard Mantel, Stan Mack, and Gil Eisner) reinvented editorial art. Conceptual illustration, which has often been credited as the invention of the *New York Times* op-ed page, was perfected five years earlier in the news and feature sections of the *Sunday Trib*. Palazzo believed that a newspaper was an amalgam of visual and written elements: "Sometimes news shapes design," he wrote, "sometimes design shapes the news." Before the *Trib*'s sad demise and doomed reincarnation as the *World Journal Tribune*, Palazzo was getting ready to mount a full-scale attack on the daily paper. "What I'd really like to do," he wrote, "is shift the whole newspaper into a magazine format—but this is still premature." He was right. Yet his revolutionary approach was the inspiration for major redesigns of the *New York Times* and the *Minneapolis Tribune* that commenced at the end of the decade.

By 1969, there was a common feeling that with the success that television was having in attracting large advertising revenues, newspapers would become extinct in the way of the great behemoth general magazines (*Collier's*, the *Saturday Evening Post*) because they could not support large circulations with small advertising revenues. The future, it seemed, was linked to the success of redesigns. As Louis Silverstein began to make inroads at that "old gray lady," the *New York Times*, in 1969, Massimo Vignelli was taking larger strides with a brand new five-section weekly newspaper called *The Herald*. Vignelli designed a rigid format with no typeface variations, only changes in point size and leading to show story hierarchy. Equally important was the fact that *The Herald* used cold type and was printed on an offset press at a time when traditional newspapers had virtually not changed technology since Gutenberg. Though it only published for a year, *The Herald* was an inspiration for other weeklies.

# Records: From Charles Ives to Janis Joplin

We know that the sixties were a decade of extremes, but nowhere was it more profound than in the music industry. So many public tastes had to be catered to that a single record company usually had an exceedingly variegated inventory of talent. Beginning in the 1940s, Columbia Records was at the forefront of progressive, popular, and classical music, as well as being a pioneer in its packaging. In the sixties it also became the preeminent purveyor of rock and roll with Bob Dylan, Janis Joplin, and the Byrds among its many luminaries. In 1960 Bob Cato, a photographer and editorial art director who had apprenticed with Alexey Brodovitch, was hired by Columbia Records president Goddard Lieberson; in 1965 he became the vice president of Creative Services. One of Cato's breakthroughs was the elimination of what had become known as the "tombstone" cover—essentially a spiritless point-of-purchase advertisement—in favor of customized art and photography. "I created an open-door policy allowing musicians and their management who for many years had no voice in the creative process of packaging to have a say," recalled Cato. "I also wanted the artists to be photographed by the best shooters in the business." He arranged for, among others, Eugene Smith to photograph Charles Ives and Fats Waller. "It wasn't that the in-house photographers were bad, but Smith, Richard Avedon, and the others brought a distinctive personality to their subjects. I was also committed to using contemporary artists, such as Robert Rauschenberg for projects like the American Music Series. And Lieberson was excited because this had never been done before."

By the mid-sixties, an album cover was a plum assignment for a graphic designer. By the late sixties, with the rock and roll renaissance in full tilt, it was a decided proving ground for exciting new ideas. "But it was also evident that the rockers wanted to do their own record covers and control their own image," said Cato about this new, challenging relationship between designer and artist. Although it appeared to outsiders that rock music and its packaging had no constraints, Cato reminds us it was very much a business: "Janis Joplin wanted R. Crumb [the San Francisco underground cartoonist who created Mr. Natural and Angel food McSpade] to do the cover of Big Brother's second album. We both loved the finished art, but I was concerned

## By the mid-sixties, an album cover was a plum assignment for a graphic designer.

that if the title was *Sex, Drugs and Cheap Thrills*, as planned, that even in those days, the album wouldn't get airplay. I asked if she would settle for just *Cheap Thrills*? I wasn't asking her to compromise—*Cheap Thrills* really said it all anyway. And Janis, in her funny, gracious way, agreed that it was better. Janis was as smart as they came, and really understood the constraints of the business."

Cato and his associate John Berg (who became vice president in the seventies) created a hothouse mentality at Columbia, allowing other talented designers (among them Henrietta Condak, Jerold Smokler, Ron Coro, Richard Mantel, Tony Lane, and Virginia Team) to push the visual form. Poster-like typography and conceptual illustration (by the likes of Philip Hayes, Milton Glaser, Cliff Condak, Robert Weaver, Paul Davis, and Nick Fasciano) were used in unprecedented ways. Contrary to the perception that many Columbia rock covers were merely fashionable or trendy, many were rather timeless in concept and execution and still hold up. Indeed, two of Cato's projects reveal the graphic diversity within this one company regarding rock and roll. When it came time to do Laura Nyro's first album, Cato, who had become her close friend, decided upon a dramatically lit photo of Nyro's downturned face. It was such a striking shot that he didn't want any copy on the cover, but rather had it printed on the shrink-wrap. It was the first time this technique had been tried, and it opened new realms of printing applications. Cato also had the greatest American iconographer, Norman Rockwell, do a cover for the "the greatest American rock duo," Mike Bloomfield and Al Kooper. At Columbia no possibility went untried.

*The rationales for corporate communications were varied. One was that if consumers are pleased with one product in the corporate family, they will try another.*

Although Columbia was not the only record company producing good music and exemplary packaging, it did so with the most consistent verve. At the zenith of American record production and sales, Columbia Records' corporate philosophy helped spark the golden age of album design.

## Building the American Corporate Image

"The case for corporate identity is being stated—and possibly overstated—with increasing frequency," wrote Patricia Allen Dreyfus in a 1969 *Print* critique. "It is invoked in the name of higher profits, greater efficiency, and improved public relations." One-fourth of the American corporations, she reported at the time, had full-time directors of corporate identity, and many others had a planned system and policy to guide identification practices. The CI field began in the mid-fifties, with Container Corporation of America (Herbert Bayer), IBM (Paul Rand), and CBS (William Golden) in the forefront; however, "total communications planning" boomed during the sixties owing to an epidemic of mergers and acquisitions that led to a large-scale identity crisis. Companies were not only merging but emerging. Over three times more corporations were doing business in the sixties than in the previous decade. Equally importantly, this was the era of diversification. "You don't need research to tell you that something that says Radio Corporation of America no longer fits a company where radios represent less than two percent of its total business and whose operations . . . now extend throughout the entire world," said RCA's director of corporate identification in a 1969 interview.

Though the practice was only a few years old, in 1968 *Fortune* magazine referred to corporate identification as "a somewhat arcane phrase." What began as a graphics problem became one of "total corporate communications," including everything from graphics and nomenclature to interiors and architecture. One firm even coined the pseudoscientific term "symbiotic" to replace the words "corporate identity," thus fueling the criticism of the corporate communications field as just a lot of mumbo jumbo. Jargon like "synergism," "system studies," "catalytic," and "quality rub-off" replaced the straightforward "that's nice" or "it works" in an attempt to give style to the emperor's new clothes. Lippincott & Margulies were the first to offer "massive research," which many critics called a dog-and-pony act designed to show clients that they were getting value for their big communications dollars.

The rationales for corporate communications were varied. One was that if consumers are pleased with one product in the corporate family, they will try another. Advocates also argued that the fiscal consequence of CI was that a company that catches the public eye will also attract investors. Many purveyors of CI believed that its primary value was internal. As an example, Dreyfus quoted from a Lippincott & Margulies promotional pamphlet entitled "Con Edison: A Troubled Giant and Its Dramatic Turnaround," which claimed that Con Ed's "clean energy" theme, devised in the sixties, offered employees a standard of excellence that encouraged them to improve the quality of company services. Perhaps more accurately, the change of slogan from "Dig We Must for a Growing New York" to "Clean Energy" on its new powder-blue trucks was really geared to turn the consumer's perception of Con Ed around from corporate foe to beneficent pal. Dreyfus, however, noted that "if you have lousy products [or services], putting Helvetica all over them isn't going to change anything."

The common complaint about CI, even back then, was that corporate symbols were too similar. "The problem facing both the manufacturer and the designer today," wrote Robert Zeidman, an industrial designer, in a 1967 *Print* article, "is how to develop a symbol that will not get lost in the crowd." One obvious solution was to avoid the many clichés that had developed. "[M]ore than 9,000 symbols in the shape of a diamond have been registered with the U.S. Patent Office," wrote Zeidman, who also said that ovals, circles, arrows, and "simplified representation of the planetary system" were too commonplace. While not discounting geometric marks, he suggested that

*"[M]ore than 9,000 symbols in the shape of a diamond have been registered with the U.S. Patent Office," wrote Zeidman, who also said that ovals, circles, arrows, and "simplified representation of the planetary system" were too commonplace.*

trade characters ultimately evoke the most powerful feelings. Admittedly, in the 1960s, this was reactionary.

Before 1961, the year that Chermayeff & Geismar's new identity for the Chase Manhattan Bank was introduced, logos for financial institutions were quite literal (e.g., the Chase National Bank logo showed a map of the USA with its founder in an oval). However, when the company merged to become the Chase Manhattan Bank (the largest banking institution in the world), Chairman David Rockefeller decided that a recognizable identity was imperative, and a unique mark was needed that would stick in the public's mind. "We showed him abstract marks like the Red Cross, as well as those beautifully simple Japanese family crests," recalls Thomas Geismar. "None of these were indicative of banking but that was not as important as achieving some distinction. Our particular design solution was actually a random selection, but one that could also be rationalized afterward as one of those foreign coins with holes in the middle." Chase's abstract mark became the archetype for banks and other multinational institutions.

Before 1964, oil companies had employed industrial designers to design gas stations, trucks, uniforms, etc. By the sixties even the best of these systems was deemed old-fashioned. When Elliot Noyes (who had brought visual order to IBM and Westinghouse) was commissioned to develop a unified program for Mobil, he collaborated with Chermayeff & Geismar on the graphics. The result was the first truly integrated plan for architectural, industrial, and graphic design for any oil company—including the development of a new logo and a radical new form for the gas pump.

Beginning in the 1940s, Container Corporation of America had been on the vanguard of progressive design in terms of its corporate identity owing to its president Walter Paepke's appreciation for modern art and the Bauhausian influence of Herbert Bayer, whom Paepke had hired as design director. John Massey, who went to CCA in 1957, continued the Bayer tradition when he became director of corporate communications in 1964. "I was attracted by the corporate philosophy that design should be integrated with industry," he says, "and with the notion that clear, crisp expression of ideas can be achieved by using type, space, color and form without reverting to superficial trends." Massey administered the Great Ideas of Western Man program; the flagship of CCA's design program, it was a landmark campaign that used a variety of design and art forms to express the company's diversity and creative approaches. Massey's design was at once timeless, yet decidedly of its time. "That is because everything was orderly. Our principal typography was Helvetica, but every once in a while, we'd go wild and use Univers." Paradoxically, the design of CCA's packaging for clients often failed to equal the high creative standards of its corporate philosophy, suggesting a troublesome dichotomy between what was deemed acceptable for institutions and salable to the public.

For Massimo Vignelli, rational corporate identification was not simply a vocation—it was a mission. In 1965, together with Chicago-based Ralph Eckerstrom (former design director of CCA), Jay Doblin, and James Fogelman, Vignelli founded Unimark to provide total communications services for international corporations. Unimark soon became multinational, with offices in the Chicago, New York, Johannesburg, and Milan, among other cities. Vignelli was zealous about "spreading the gospel" of graphic discipline. "I believed that the emphasis on individualism, and the lack of discipline prevalent in design at the time was wreaking havoc on graphic communications and hampering the access of information." Helvetica and the grid were his tools of preference; order and objectivity were his credo. Accordingly, members of the firm were required to wear white lab coats.

## Making the Environment Better

One of the most complex commissions awarded to Unimark and Vignelli came out of the 1966 decision to unify New York City subway signage and maps, which had gone untouched since the three independent train lines were formed into the Transit Authority in 1940. "Plunged into ugliness, inundated by a jumbled spectacle of misinformation," wrote John Lahr, "the subway rider is a victim of poor city planning, his own anxieties magnified by the despairing confusion around him." Making the environment easier to navigate was the ministry Vignelli wanted to serve. However, the result was, in John Lahr's words, "a complete fiasco. The Authority sought [Unimark's] advice only to implement it without a true understanding of the total design concept."

The plan, by Vignelli and Bob Noorda, was designed to eliminate redundant information by coordinating all signage and graphic standards. The principle, Vignelli recalled, "was to give the information only at the point of decision—never before, never after." They developed a modular system of sign panels that would suspend from special channels. "In our plan," explained Vignelli, "we had drawn a black strip to represent the channel into which each panel would fit. But they [the Authority, who appropriated some of the plan but did not have enough sense to let Unimark do the execution] misunderstood and painted this black strip across each sign as part of the visual image." Vignelli said at the time, "the wrong approach is to do [this] on a democratic basis."

Interestingly, a concurrent commission, awarded to Walter Kacik by the New York Sanitation Commissioner to modernize the department's trucks and signs, gave total control to the designer. His efforts at standardizing signs and trucks were well received until his patron, the commissioner, resigned and the program lost momentum.

Black Rock, CBS's imposing Manhattan headquarters, is a prominent example of total design control. "The traditional emphasis that CBS places on quality and taste in design is symbolized by its striking new building," wrote Irwin Rothman in a 1966 analysis. "Both William S. Paley, chairman of the board, and Frank Stanton, president of CBS, saw the building as an unparalleled opportunity to create a distinguished, unified expression of the corporate personality." Louis Dorfsman was asked to design the entire

*Making the environment easier to navigate was the ministry Vignelli wanted to serve. However, the result was, in Lahr's words, "a complete fiasco. The Authority sought [Unimark's] advice only to implement it without a true understanding of the total design concept."*

graphics program, from lobby graphics (the main typeface was a modified Didot and a secondary face a modified Helvetica called CBS-Sans Serif) to the top-floor restaurant. With the Paley-Stanton dictum "no detail is too small to warrant serious attention," the reason for Dorfsman's total involvement is clear: "Allowing a contractor to dictate the use of typography on structures," he said in 1966, "has generally resulted in a low standard . . . for most buildings." Indeed, every detail, including the clock face and numerals on elevator buttons, was specifically designed. About the uncommon and decidedly elegant use of Didot, he said, "I could have resorted to the obvious use of a strong typeface. But instead I took the opposite course and chose the elegant delicacy of Didot . . . set against the strong, bold quality of the building created a desirable counterpoint." Rothman concluded that "the CBS building clearly serves as an example of what can be accomplished when top management seriously attempts to coordinate and integrate building design with good graphics." One should add that without a design autocrat like Dorfsman, even the best intentions could, and have, gone sour.

*Psychedelia, which connotes a drug-induced, mind-expanding state, was really a people's art, a rejection of the staid typographic and pictorial vocabulary of "officialdom" for a universal sensory experience.*

## Anarchy: Fashion or Philosophy?

One might think that no two design methods could be more dissimilar than the corporate and psychedelic styles, but there are curious similarities. The former is about conveying information precisely, while the latter is about transmitting an aura instantaneously. Both use graphic means to symbolize an ethic or point of view. In fact, one of the leading San Francisco poster artists was taught at Yale by ex-Bauhaus master Josef Albers. Victor Moscoso, who had more classical design training than many traditional designers, says of Albers's influence on the psychedelic poster, "I had vibrating colors down pat. I thought it was some kind of Zen meditation trip at the time, it was driving me crazy. But I did store it. So, by the time that a situation presented itself where I was able to use that information, it was like a having . . . an oil well on your property."

The psychedelic poster, as designed by Mouse and Kelly, Rick Griffin and Wes Wilson, primarily as an announcement for the San Francisco concert halls, was a unique language based on old forms. "We took from any and all sources," Moscoso continues. "The world was our swipe file. Any image was *our* image.

All we had to do was put it in a different context." Psychedelia, which connotes a drug-induced, mind-expanding state, was really a people's art, a rejection of the staid typographic and pictorial vocabulary of "officialdom" for a universal sensory experience. One needn't be stoned to read these generational signposts. Once decoded, the language of psychedelia was simple. "These posters worked," says Moscoso, "because they were not encumbered by the rules of 'good design.' The rule that a 'poster should transmit a message simply and quickly' became 'how long can you engage the viewer in reading.' 'Don't use vibrating colors' became 'use them whenever you can and irritate the eyes as much as you can.' 'Lettering should always be legible' changed to 'disguise the lettering as much as possible.' After all, the musicians had turned up their amps *to kill* . . . so I turned up the amps on my color so that every edge vibrated."

Within a year of its inception, psychedelic art became a national craze, with some good (and mostly bad) imitators working at full gear. Moscoso, dumbfounded by how quickly the commercial society ate it up and spit it out, turned his attention to underground comix. With his poster peers, as well as cartoonists R. Crumb, S. Clay Wilson, Gilbert Shelton, and others, he published *Zap Comix* in 1969. It was the granddaddy of the form, featuring an exciting array of graphic approaches used to present many taboo subjects, including the most taboo—incest. Moscoso notes that this time the establishment wasn't so quick to co-opt: "They drew the line at incest." The graphic inspiration for these comix came from prewar comic books, Tijuana Bibles, and pulp magazines. But the ribald and sacrilegious content of the underground comix was born in the early fifties in Harvey Kurtzman's *Mad* magazine and raised to new heights of creative anarchy by young cartoonists who spoke for the hippies, yippies, Aquarians, and all the other baby-boomer kids of the sixties.

Before there were underground comix, the strips appeared in a variety of underground newspapers—some which published for many years, and others that were fly-by-night operations. The most venerable were the *Los Angeles Free Press* and the *Berkeley Barb*, but the most famous was the *East Village Other*, which began to publish in 1965 on the Lower East Side of New York. *EVO*, as it was known, had an ad hoc format that changed regularly according to whoever was laying out its pages. Its covers were often surrealistic photomontages in the manner of the German Dadaists, while

*What the underground represented in the sixties was merely the surface. The real design advances were tied to the mainstream.*

its insides were collages of pictorial debris from all over the lot, as well as full-page comic strips by Crumb, Spain Rodriguez, Kim Deitch, and others. Realizing that *EVO* was filling a void created by the fact that no "official" publications existed for the growing youth market, record companies began inserting fashionably designed advertisements that provided a stunning counterpoint to the anarchic layout. *EVO*, which continued to publish (albeit in emasculated form) until 1972, was the bridge between a real counterculture and today's more trendy culture tabloids.

## Typography: Expression, not Compression

Saul Bass was interested in the ideas presented in György Kepes's book *Language of Vision* (1944). "He had an embracing point of view about art, which I had never encountered before." Bauhaus thought was a foundation for most, not the rule.

At the same time, Aspen became the headquarters for post-Bauhaus design applications. Chicago, the rational, or late modern, approach began in the mid-1950s. Its exponents were influenced to a certain extent by the Bauhaus and Swiss and Italian rational movements, but were decidedly

American in terms of the style of imagery and typography. They represented the "type that speaks" period of American design.

## The Sixties: Over in Our Lifetime?

The underground is dead, but if it had lived it wouldn't have stayed underground. Just look at *Rolling Stone*. A product of the youth culture, it has ebbed and flowed with the vicissitudes of politics and culture, and today it is a well-designed and edited chronicle of current events. What the underground represented in the sixties was merely the surface. The real design advances were tied to the mainstream. So what has happened to these manifestations?

Many of the designers who injected new life into American practice are still practicing. Quite a few of the magazines still publish, and many of the corporate identities continue today. However, have the lessons of this mature period of American design been carried on? Now that television has drained the advertising talent, is print as well done as before? Now that MBAs have become middlepersons in business and corporate design programs, can creativity still flower? Now that mega design firms are forced by economic necessity to make high profits, will design become more service-oriented? Perhaps we will see in the next two chapters. But what is undeniable is that the sixties (as we've defined it) was a dramatic period during which technological inventions and conceptual innovations converged to form a distinctively American design profession—one that had never been seen before.

Originally published in *Print* magazine, November–December 1989.

# DISCUSSION POINTS

- What key values distinguish the 1960s from all other design periods?
- Can a decade neatly define styles or attitudes of design?
- What were the most important aesthetic and philosophical lessons of the period?
- Will one aspect of 1960s design stand out above all others?

*There are so many small design tricks, motifs, and conceits that comprise the designer's tool kit. This collection of some of them were compiled for a short column, "Evolution," that I did for* Print *magazine from the mid-1990s to the early 2000s.*

# Evolution of Design Conceits

## Street Sign Typography

I challenge anyone to produce the name of the first designer to co-opt a street sign as a design motif. Whoever it was started one of the most ubiquitous of all conceits to be found on record, book, and magazine covers and countless other graphic wares. Paul Rand, Saul Bass, and countless other moderns did it. The earliest example I found, from the mid-1920s, was created by an anonymous hack illustrator for the jacket of a melodrama that takes place in Old New York. Scores followed. Yet even though parodying street sign typography has become cliché, it still crops up often. The film titles for Spike

Lee's 1991 *Jungle Fever*, designed by Randy Balsmeyer, are made from an array of street signs. More recently, B. Middleworth's (of Bats4bones Design Inc.) Photoshop-rendered jacket for the 2005 true crime expose *Desire Street* is made from signs on a traffic light stanchion. The street sign motif never gets tired—perhaps because it is such a quick problem-solver, it will never be retired. Just look at the July 2005 cover of *Time Out New York* for the latest sign of the times.

## The Eyes Have It

In the 1950s, Walter and Margaret Keane started a craze for "Big Eye," also known as "Waif," "Sad Eye," or "Keane Eye," paintings featuring waiflike children with large, globular, and dewy sad eyes, pathetically dressed in rags or clown togs and otherwise awkwardly posed to exact sympathy from the viewer. Like the proverbial train wreck, this syrupy representational art was so prosaic it was mesmerizing. The prints were hauntingly ubiquitous in living and bedrooms throughout America for decades, until one day the fickle finger of taste turned toward other things cute, like little doe-eyed deer and diaper-clad baby chimps. In an instant the Keane Eyes were, for the moment at any rate, relegated to the kitsch bin of history. Yet Keane's art (Margaret was the real inventor of the style) retains, for some, such contemporary cultural cachet that its influence has evolved into a commercial hipster style, extremely popular in Japanese manga, art by Takashi Murakami, and most recently in American illustration (see the advertisement for Screaming Mimis) and cool stock art (CSA Archive), where copies of the originals abound. There's no accounting for taste, but the age of irony begat the age of kitsch, which begat the age of anything for a chuckle, and so Keane's characters, practiced by the acolytes, have retaken the high/low ground.

## The Rays Have It

"Getting some rays," for graphic designers, is more than a euphemism for soaking up the sun. It also means exploiting one of the hottest clichés in the proverbial design stylebook. Rays are in (as if they were ever out). And other than the simple graphic dominance emitted, the reason for their ubiquity, mostly in movie posters, remains something of a mystery. Perhaps designers are simply paying homage to the Japanese Rising Sun Flag, also known as "Hi-no-maru" or "sun disc." Used in ancient Japan by the shoguns of Tokugawa, the sun represented ultimate dominion and inexhaustible power. But why Will Ferrell or chubby dancing pandas or even *Zombie Strippers* are juxtaposed to radiating rays suggests a more practical rationale. It is hard to ignore this hypnotic image when used as the backdrop for a heroic pose.

## Two-Faced Design

It is no mystery why the Italian Futurist artist Renato Bertelli sculpted *Profilo Continuo del Duce* (1933). But there is a real question why Karim Rashid used the exact same image, albeit illuminated, for the cover of his recent book *Karim Rashid: Evolution*, which he calls "Ego Vase." Futurists celebrated speed and the Fascist dictatorship of Benito Mussolini, their futuristic leader. And despite calling themselves "Futurists," they also retained a guarded appreciation of the ancient past, if only as fuel for irony. Bertelli's *Profilo* is a tip of the hat to Janus, the Roman god of beginnings and endings (thus the reason it is a double-faced head staring in opposite directions). Like Mussolini, Janus was worshipped at the beginning of life's key transitions, like the seasons, and also represented such opposites as war and peace. Futurists enjoyed playing with opposites and invested static art and photography, like *Profilo* and *Photodynamic Umberto Boccioni* by Giannetto Bisi, with the illusion of speed. These twirling, two-faced heads were actually a common means of expressing motion. Rashid's plastic reworking of Bertelli's wood sculpture also symbolizes speed, but anyone who recognizes that the face originally belonged to the infamous Mussolini must wonder why this original designer borrowed this particularly dubious visage.

## Design in the Shadows

Creating shadows is among the most popular Photoshop tools. Shadows simulate three-dimensionality in 2-D space, and designers are happiest when they can simulate things that might but do not exist. Shadows are a perfect way to make the real surreal. Why else have shadow plays, especially the common making of animals and beasts from hand-shadows, been so popular in life and in art, and for so long? Shadows also provide other dimensions, including drama and mystery. Noir cinema is entirely rooted in the manipulation of light to create dramatic shadows. B-movie posters of the 1930s and '40s graphically replicated these cinematic shadows for maximum effect. Today's film posters are rife with the shadow conceit. The teaser promotion for *The X -Files* shows an aerial view of Mulder and Scully casting shadows in the shape of an X. *The Legend of God's Gun* ("A rock n' roll spaghetti western") has a priest casting a shadow that turns into a cross. And *Taxi to the Dark Side* (a film about rendition and torture in Afghanistan) eerily transforms shadows into an American flag. In each of these instances, shadows become something other, another way of graphically conveying a layered message in an economical—indeed eye-catching and mind-expanding—way.

## Lines, Arrows, Dots, and Modernism

There is something comforting about how early American modernist designers like Rand, Lustig, and McKnight Kauffer borrowed what we might call old-fashioned classic images—like Greek or Roman sculpture—then guilelessly combined them with glyph-like schematic lines, arrows, and dots. These modernists saw themselves as perpetuating timelessness; classic ideals of proportion and beauty were symbolized through updated vintage graphic artifacts and used to construct a futuristic graphic language. Now this all appears nostalgically dated, but nonetheless still comforting. Richard Turtletaub regularly delves into the modernist toolbox to as if to carry the torch of this evolutionary progression. His sometimes retrofitted work is starkly reminiscent of those designers mentioned above, as well as 1940s and '50s modernists, Matthew Leibowitz and György Kepes among others. "I like the multi-layered, torn, bold, graphic quality to photogram cover for *Cahiers D'Art* by Kepes," admits Turtletaub. "There's something about the energy and the abstract/fine art aspect within this piece that I wanted to bring into my own work." There is also something curiously naïf about these lines, arrows, and dots, as though they are passed down from more sophisticated times.

## Follow the Arrows

In 288 the future St. Sebastian, the son of a wealthy Roman family converted to Christianity, was tied to a tree, shot with arrows, and left for dead. He survived, recovered, returned to preach the gospel, and converted, among others, Roman soldiers and a governor to the faith. He was canonized for his miracle. (During the fourteenth century, when the Black Death was referred to as being shot by an army of nature's archers, celebrants prayed to St. Sebastian because of his brush with those slings and arrows.) When in 1969 George Lois adopted St. Sebastian as the metaphor for his first Muhammad Ali cover of *Esquire*, the rationale was simple: Ali had been stripped of his heavyweight titles for refusing to participate in the Vietnam War, given his religious convictions, and was thus a martyr for the cause of peace. (Incidentally, since St. Sebastian was Christian, Ali was reluctant to pose this way without permission from Elijah Muhammad, leader of the Nation of Islam—he received it.) Lois didn't know at the time that the metaphor had a deeper meaning. Just as St. Sebastian survived, so too did Ali as an American icon. The cover also survived. It was recently ranked the third greatest magazine cover of the past forty years by the American Society of Magazine Editors (ASME) and has also become an icon in its own right— copied on posters and magazine covers, most recently the decidedly less poignant *Radar* send-up of Tom Cruise.

## Blinders

Noir films of the 1930s and '40s featured shadowy characters peering through dark window blinds as a common melodramatic trope. Mirko Ilic's American flag blinds, behind which is revealed a pair of menacing blue eyes, illustrated a 2001 *New York Times Book Review* cover story about biological terrorism and was indeed dramatic, Now it is also a common trope. Published one month after the attacks of 9/11 and during the ensuing anthrax scares, the editors hotly debated if it would be too disturbing for readers, but decided to run with it because it was startling. It was also all-purpose. Ilic even subsequently produced a slightly different version (without the flag) for Samantha Power's *A Problem from Hell: America and the Age of Genocide*, a book criticizing our ineffectual government policy. A year later, a similar image, though not done by Ilic, appeared on the cover of a book devoted to spying. And recently, to commemorate the fifth anniversary of 9/11, virtually the same image, again not by Ilic, was published in different advertisements in the same edition of the *New York Times*. One was promoting the TV movie *The Path to 9/11*, showing eyes gazing out from cut-out stripes of the flag (though not literally a blind, it's the same idea), and the other, for *The Price of Security*, a TV documentary, follows Ilic's blinds motif. A similar image, photographed in February 2006 by Bumper DeJesus, is currently available on Corbis.

## The Swash Is Back (Squiggly by Any Other Name)

Art nouveau began when *graphistes*, rebelling against the rapid urban growth in the wake of the Industrial Revolution, replaced turgid academic art with exotic, curvilinear decoration, replete with vines and tendrils that wrapped around everything from typefaces to furniture, like Hector Guimard's Paris Metro Station entrances. At its peak in the early 1900s, so-called floriated madness emerged as the symbol of a youthful exuberance, but after becoming an international style until the outbreak of World War I, it was destined for mediocrity as well. The style made a huge comeback as psychedelic poster art in the late 1960s, yet once again it experienced a short shelf life. Since designers have a congenital love/hate relationship with ornament (moderns despise it, eclectics celebrate it), art nouveau has gone in and out of fashion as quickly as paisley prints. These days, however, vegetative-styled ornament is back in the news, incorporating other kinds of swashes, swirls, spirals, and florid decorative effluvia, like the recent poster/advertisement for Passion Bait by Tank, which has brought one good old turn-of-the-twentieth-century look in to the brand new twenty-first.

## Revolving Around Beardsley

During the psychedelic sixties, when graphic artists reprised past styles from Victorian to art nouveau to deco, the English *graphiste* and erotic *symboliste* Aubrey Beardsley (1872–1898), the so-called "dandy of the grotesque," was posthumously returned from his exile in the artistic wilderness. His excessive curvilinear style and chiaroscuro sexual fantasies were a potent antidote to austere modernist design. His style also was a particularly apt influence on drug-inspired hippie aesthetics of the day. But it was the Beatles who inadvertently made Beardsley more popular than during his own lifetime. The 1966 release of their landmark album *Revolver* featured a quirky cover portrait of the group by Klaus Voormann that combined Beardsley-esque linear styling (especially the obsessive lines that composed the Beatles' hair) with collaged silhouetted photos of the "lads" culled from various stages of their musical lives. This single piece of art altered the way LP sleeves would be designed for the next decade. Beatle fans (and Beatle-ologists) dissected every aspect of the cover for hidden meanings. The black-and-white cover was at once haunting and comforting, polished and raw, yet decidedly unlike any other pop record sleeves (usually straight photographic portraits of bands) that preceded it. Soon afterward Beardsley-original and Beardsley-inspired illustrations cropped up in abundance on rock posters, underground newspapers, and hippie ephemera. But the Beardsley veneration was short-lived. While his life and work continue to interest scholars and collectors, by the mid-1970s it was passé to copy the style. In 2005, however, a Milan-based online periodical called *This Is A Magazine* (www.thisisamagazine.com/) published a cover slavishly influenced by *Revolver*, if not Beardsley himself. And this is only one of various homages that include a recent Microsoft Windows ad in the *New Yorker* and an album cover for the band LB, *Pop Artificielle*.

## Dadamation

Few early twentieth-century art forms are more enduring or alluring for style-mongering designers than Dada and Russian Constructivism, which may account for why so many of us reprise the collages made by German Dadaists Hannah Hoch or Raoul Haussmann, or the Russian film posters by the Stenberg brothers and Gustav Klutsis, in an overabundance of contemporary print compositions. But now that's old school. What's new is a spate of totally delightful Dada and Constructivist remixes recently produced for the large and small screen. In 2006, the rockers Franz Ferdinand, whose CD graphics frequently reference Dada and Bauhaus graphics, produced "Take Me Out," an animated and live-action music video smartly referencing a medley of Hausmann, Francis Picabia, Alexander Rodchenko, and other modernist inspirations. That same year, Trollback + Company cleverly snipped together and animated various Stenberg movie posters for a Turner Classic Movies on-air bumper. And in 2006, to introduce Stolyi vodka's latest avant garde–inspired ad campaign, a hybrid of Lissitzky and Rodchenko typography comes alive on the TV screen. In the evolution of design pastiche, animation breathes new life into these classic old forms.

## Spread Them Legs

Among arthropods and vertebrates, the leg has evolved several times over as many eons. Initially its evolution was intelligently designed to facilitate locomotion underwater, then for movement over land. However, on book covers and film and theater posters, the spread leg (or legs), used as a dramatic and comic framing device for ancillary images, appears not to have evolved very much at all. In fact, it is the most frequently copied trope ever used. From steamy pulp paperbacks, designed in the '40s to titillate male fantasies, to ham-fisted movie advertisements designed today to captivate anyone's attention, nary a year has gone by without at least one version of the cut-off-torso-spread-leg perspective. So when did it begin? Some early nineteenth-century engravings show spread-legged evil types lording over cowering victims. In westerns, one duelist seen through the legs of the other is the quintessential showdown stance. Mid-twentieth-century pulp magazine covers were known for recoiling women seen through the legs of menacing men (or seen through the legs of sultry women in the case of lesbian pulps). Eventually, the conceit was used to frame all manner of melodrama and comedy, from James Bond to Austin Powers to the lawman in the recent *3:10 to Yuma*. This motif surely has legs.

Originally published in various issues of *Print* magazine in the mid-1990s to the early 2000s.

## DISCUSSION POINTS

- What are some design conceits not discussed here?
- Are conceits always clichés?
- What is a cliché?

# TWO: DESIGN DIALECTS

Illustration began, more or less, with the Egyptian slaves who drew anthropomorphic caricatures of their masters on tiny pieces of papyrus, illustrating in metaphor the sadistic ogres who lorded over them. Jump a couple millennia or so to eighteenth-century Europe to see that that same satiric impulse is embedded in illustrators' genomes. The legendary British caricaturists James Gilray, Thomas Rowlandson, and William Hogarth improved greatly upon the ancient slaves' scribbles with more accurate, wittier depictions of human foibles, but showing their target's buffoonery came from the same need.

# Illustration: From Then to Now and Back Again

Illustration has changed radically since the eighteenth century and into the nineteenth, when cartoon and caricature were the means of social and political critique, but in many ways it has not changed at all. Constant is the artist's desire to convey or illuminate a message and tell a story through whichever means—realistic or abstract, expressive or impressionistic—will do the job. What does evolve, however (aside from changes in context), is the style of illustration.

History reveals three significant truths:

1. Illustration styles shift back and forth, so old becomes new, new becomes old.

2. Certain illustration styles brand an era (Charles Dana Gibson's linear "Gibson Girl" style is forever wed to the turn of the century Gilded Age; J. C. Leyendecker's Arrow shirt is unmistakably 1920s; Stevan Dohanos's *Saturday Evening Post* covers are late 1940s and early '50s).

3. Illustrators have personal visual styles (or personalities) that transcend the moment (Seymour Chwast, Robert Grossman, and R. O. Blechman bridge many stylistic eras with their distinctive styles). Although each of these styles may incorporate traits from other evolutionary periods, they have made it their own.

Nonetheless, there are definitely overarching styles that reflect a historical moment and evolved into current fashion. Here are a few:

The Victorian style (last quarter of the nineteenth century), at times eerie and absurd, realistic and idealistic, fanciful and farcical, and always intricate and layered, was typified by darkly ornate mannerisms produced in black-and-white ink line and brush and steel engravings or woodcuts. Victorians were decorous on the outside but bawdy under the surface. Likewise, Victorian book and magazine illustration was often turgidly formalistic yet conceptually freewheeling, running the gamut from incredible fantasy to biting satire, with many shades of black and gray in between. The Victorian era was the bridge between the Industrial Revolution and the modern twentieth century, and its distinctive illustration and design endures as symbolic of these times. This passé style was brought back in the 1960s,

## World War I put an abrupt end to all forms of ephemeral excess.

most notably by Edward Gorey, whose appropriate last name underscored his lovingly ironic use of the tropes of Victorianism.

By the early 1890s, academic realism was under attack by movements of artists known by different names throughout Europe—L'Art Nouveau in France, La Libre Esthetique in Belgium, Stile Liberty (or Stile Inglese) in Italy, Secession in Austria, Modernista in Spain, Jugendstil in Germany, the Glasgow School in Scotland, and the Bohemian Secession in Czechoslovakia—and in America, as practiced by Will Bradley and Maxfield Parrish, it was a rose by any other name, called art nouveau. Its floreated ornamental tropes spread tentacles everywhere art was made.

The style is a marker of the revolution in poster design as it was practiced in Paris, with Toulouse-Lautrec, Jules Chéret, and Alphonse Mucha. Art nouveau signaled a social and cultural realignment. Its practitioners were linked by their shared belief that "the total work of art" was not merely found on canvas or sculpted out of marble but rather extended to a range of functional products—including illustration.

World War I put an abrupt end to all forms of ephemeral excess. And after the war, other styles that had briefly emerged as alternatives to art nouveau became dominant:

Expressionism erupted in Germany in 1905 during a tumultuous epoch when Europe was facing social and political revolutions. Expressionism was a movement of rebellious painters and graphic artists who repudiated the academic tenets and conventional methods of making formal art. The proponents drew upon primitive iconography, not the least of which were

African totems and masks. Deformation of the figure was employed to heighten the intensity of expression.

Expressionists became illustrators to reach a mass audience. Frans Masereel's wordless pictorial narratives (the precursor to the graphic novel) captured the torment of man and the horror and monumentality of the World War.

After the war, illustrators continued to pursue a kind of "artistic truth," opening the floodgates for artists to break the classical rules of draftsmanship. That legacy continues to this day.

Another alternative, art deco, introduced in Paris in 1925, was a decorative approach to the human form that simplified and stylized all physical objects, injecting an aura of streamlined elegance. For the most part, the style relied on patterns made up of reductive ornamentation. The airbrush was the defining tool because it enabled artists to create textures made from line, mass, and shadow that had a smooth veneer that evoked the sense of motion. The airbrush was used to soften the hard edges, resulting in modeled, sculptural rendering. Illustrators took the opportunity to be haute courant. Deco was an instantly identifiable graphic code.

Deco, furthermore, emerged simultaneously in almost every industrialized nation. The style signaled progress and suggested the future. As illustration, it was a key motif in advertisements for automobiles, railway cars and engines, airplanes, furniture, appliances, liquor, and, of course, fashion—anything that could be stylized was imbued with sophistication. A. M. Cassandre was not a narrative illustrator per se, yet he incorporated painting and drawing into his poster designs for Au Bucheron, Dubonnet, and Nord Express. Rockwell Kent was another torchbearer. A dedicated illustrator, his stylized pen-and-ink vignettes of heroically posed men and women wed a classical sense of formal composition to contemporary nuance. It is that sense of elegance and heroism that many "retro" illustrators have appropriated over the past two decades.

The most repeated style was and is surrealism. Founded by André Breton in 1924, surrealism was a reaction to Expressionism (and Dada) with the goal of plumbing the deeper recesses of the subconscious mind. Yet surrealistic illustration was created long before the movement was constituted. The macabre cartoons by French caricaturist J. J. Grandville, circa 1850, prefigured contemporary science fiction art and provided a unique vehicle for making political and social commentary during a censorious period in French history. But Grandville was not alone—other cartoonists and illustrators were interested in fantasy and so engaged in dislocated and dreamlike imagery, which paved the way for a language of surrealism. By the late 1930s, surrealism had become a fashion, the vernacular for many commercial artists in various disciplines. Both mysterious and accessible, surrealism provided a means to visually express complex ideas, sometimes in a simplistic manner.

While Salvador Dalí was the most notorious of the surrealists, René Magritte was more influential on a larger group of illustrators. His work provided the later twentieth-century illustrator with logically illogical discordant objects to share center stage. Birds could fly on the ground, while statues could move like animate objects and humans could appear as flowers. In the surreal world, nothing followed rules of proportion or composition. Surrealism remains one of the most commonly used dialects of illustration.

All the new styles and radical conceits to the contrary, representational style—realism itself—is still the most common illustrative language. Representation can be a snapshot in time, or a manufactured scene presented as a flawlessly true depiction. The figure is key. Representation can be calm, even banal; dramatic, even monumental. It can be witty, even sarcastic. But never deliberately abstract. The god of representation is in the details. And the representative of god is none other than Norman Rockwell. For him and his disciples, mastery of light and shadow are essential elements in creating verisimilitude. Exacting precision is necessary in rendering the human form, architectural structure, and plant or tree. Representation is about making the image accessible to all through the most fundamental of realistic traits. Despite the fashions for raw *art brut* and comic art these days, representation is alive.

An offshoot of representation worth mentioning is the pulp style. It evolved from the late nineteenth century and offered a sense of melodrama with the hint of terror. Science fiction was popular (including outer space monsters), as was futurism (*Popular Science* and *Popular Mechanics* covers routinely featured the most incredible things-to-come). In fact, some of these pulps prefigured the oddities of the surrealist movement. Much of this style of illustration reflected heightened social anxieties based on headlines in the news. Pulps enabled the audience to read about and see the unthinkable in the comfort of their easy chairs.

In addition, there are some subcategories that find their way into contemporary approaches, including heroic, which relies on establishing credible myths made vivid through romantic or melodramatic pseudo-realism. Cartoon expressionism is not so much a visual style as a persistent attitude that spanned the nineteenth and twentieth centuries and appeared in periodicals. Cartoon expressionism has a brutish cast; whether finely crafted or wantonly untutored, graphic distortion—radical or subtle—is commonly used to disrupt the viewer's perceptions and make the image seductive.

These are the principal styles, the DNA of most illustrative practice. They have evolved through revival, expropriation, and transmutation to comprise the body and soul of contemporary illustration.

_____

Originally published as short columns in various issues of *Print* magazine in the 2000s.

# DISCUSSION POINTS

- What is the distinction between illustration and illumination?
- Should illustration be literal, figurative, symbolic, or allegoric?
- What does an illustrator contribute to a text?
- Should illustration exist to complement or supplement a story? Or does it merely decorate?

# The Play Principle: Paul Rand and Graphic Design

No matter how serious the intent of any design project, it must inevitably begin without constraints but with the freedom that derives from unfettered playfulness. Play underpins and increases graphic design's significance as mass communications and popular culture. About what he dubbed "The Play Instinct," Paul Rand, the influential American advertising, poster, and logo designer, stated in a 1990 interview (with me): "Without play, there would be no Picasso. Without play, there is no experimentation."[1] He emphatically added that without experimentation there is no "quest for answers." Whether in painting or typography, an artist must continually search for answers to a wide range of problems, including how to have an intimate connection with the receiver of the message—the audience. Play, as a means of discovery, is a key to surprise, and audiences love surprises.

I love quoting Paul Rand because he was such a passionate and joyous member of the generation of postwar modern designers who elevated graphic design from a methodical service to a methodical art. From the mid-1940s through the 1960s, the modernists imbued advertising and products, periodicals and books with a je ne sais quoi—the personal quirks— which provided the eye- and mind-grabbing power to pull their audience into a message. Graphic design is more than routinized hawking and selling through predictable types and staid images. There has long been an element of wit and humor found in graphic design dating back to before the turn of the century when graphic design began, but it was sporadic, ad hoc, and highly uneven until the early to mid-twentieth century, when modernism brought to the fore the work of many more designers who believed graphic design's mission was to make the world both a better and happier place in which to live. Play played a playful role in this goal.

Any graphic designer who says that play is not an essential aspect of the design process is telling a big fat lie. How can anyone so involved in the analog or digital practice of cutting, pasting, and composing letters, pictures, shapes, and patterns reject play as a fundamental behavior? Certainly, designers want to be taken seriously by businesses and all that, but play is not intended to belittle the creative conceiver/producer of printed material that surrounds us every day in every corner of our material world—it is essential to our daily life. Graphic design is not a rote activity made on a production line but a series of trials and errors derived from play.

Bringing order to chaos is, strictly speaking, the definition of design. But the truth is that without play, design is nothing but a tight blueprint.

---

[1]  Interview on the "play instinct" in: Steven Heller and Gail Anderson, *Graphic Wit: The Art of Humor in Design*, 1st ed (New York: Watson-Guptill, 1991).

It must be a tabula rasa. Of course, blueprints, templates, schematics, or other guidelines are necessary when creating design for corporate identity and branding systems. Yet before these standards are carved into commandments, first comes play—the unknown and non-preconceived.

"I use the term play," Rand explained, "but I mean coping with the problems of form and content, weighing relationships, establishing priorities. Every problem of form and constant is different, which dictates that the rules of the game are different too." That said, Rand and others in the playground do not enter into play, as he noted, "unwittingly." It is endemic to the design process, and whether it's called play or some other term, "one just does it."

Play is the gateway behavior. Play defines children as children, but many adults—professionals in many fields—engage in serious play too, including musicians, actors, artists, and athletes. Play and work are life's natural dichotomies. Yet the word "play" implies sophisticated activity. The virtuoso, master, or maestro does not reach his level of expertise through intuitive play alone. Tinkering, which is another form of play, will lead to invention and revelation, and with graphic design, playing (sketching, cutting and pasting, rendering, iterating, whatever the terminology) is that essential first step in decision making. Playing also is the foundation of the idea, which is the most essential outcome of any playful act.

A graphic designer, like any artist or craftsperson, is free to play indefinitely, but the outcome must be consequential. The role of what is imprecisely known as commercial art (as distinguished from fine art) is to convey and clarify information of various types, using image, typography, and layout as the means. On this playing field, the goal is an idea, and an idea is a combination of visuals and words or some mnemonic that resonates with the receiver. Regardless of how artful the result is—in other words, how much stylish veneer is applied to the final result—graphic design's sole purpose is to foster understanding. If in the end it goes unheeded, it has failed its job.

It is said that play is a means to an end. It should never be an end in itself but the foundation for stronger concepts. Yet even this rule of thumb has its pitfalls. There are designers, for instance, who may mistake play for something more deliberately formal or tried and true. "The visual message which professes to be profound or elegant often boomerangs as mere pretention,"

Rand warned, noting that when play leads to self-consciousness it is doomed. His rule of thumb was always simple: "I like things that are happy; I like things that will make the client smile." One role of design is to make its consumers feel better about what they consume.

Paul Rand did this in spades. He was only one of many, but his work offers a valuable starting point. Sometimes play is on the surface of the work. By this I mean, in Rand's case, his advertisements and package designs for El Producto cigars that integrate comic drawings with common photographs of the product—the cigar. Sigmund Freud is attributed with the quote, "sometimes a cigar is just a cigar" (it is not clear that he did, in fact, utter these words), but it is a fact that after playing with a few ideas, Rand took the cigar photos and added drawings of arms, legs, shoes, hats, etc., that made each one into a particular cartoon character. Rather than making the cigar into a cartoon character, he used a straight-on representational photograph of cigars and sketched or grafted human props onto and around it. This did not distort or make the product cute, but retained its realism while adding personalities. In this way he created a weekly serial or situational comedy starring the variously sized and shaped cigars interacting with one another. Although this was not a child-appropriate product, Rand's lighthearted approach made the campaign into a comic fantasy world. Like the best children's stories, he engaged the audience in a narrative that increased their anticipation for what came next. This extended from weekly newspaper advertisements to special holiday boxes and tins. This was a radical departure compared to stereotypical, formulaic cigar promotion. It was a departure influenced by modern artists like Paul Klee and Joan Miró, who had the foresight to reject conventionally accepted representational art to a highly tuned naivety.

I recall there were common critiques of modern art during the 1950s and '60s: "My five-year-old could have done this." Ha! But could their dear five-year-old develop a series of playful scenarios that so captivated the consuming public? Although Rand and others of his ilk, designers like Alvin Lustig, Saul Bass, Leo Lionni, Seymour Chwast, Milton Glaser, Cipe Pineles, and more, may have borrowed aspects of their art and design language from children—in truth, they may have never grown up—still they understood how to adapt, transform, and ultimately use these aspects to make complex statements accessible. They understood that rather than blindly accepting academic rigors of ultra-formal art and design, there were other more primal, expressive ways of making images and words jump off the page and into the hearts and minds of the receiver.

Following rules rarely produces originality; experimentation is essential (even if it fails). Play enters unknown territory. "It is the driving force of the creative spirit," Rand said, although he also said that "creative" is an abused word. "[It] is sensitive to change and the changeless. It focuses not only on what is right, but on what is exceptional."

Recently, I coauthored a book with Greg D'Onofrio titled *The Moderns* (Abrams Books), which showcases sixty-three of the mid-century modernists who, until we began assembling work for this book, I believed were lockstep in what is known as the International Style, a Swiss-based, Bauhaus-inspired view of design that, from my nearsighted perspective, denied the virtues of play and improvisation. Oh, was I wrong. Although there are decidedly similarities between work by, say, Rand, Lester Beall, Walter Allner, and Herbert Bayer, among others, there are differences in the ways they played with the elements of design and the concepts they were tasked to address. It was clear through the juxtaposition of pictures and words, the colors and overlays and geometries and abstractions, that each was making a form of visual jazz—and what is jazz but playful improvisation?

Originally published in *Serious Play: Design in Midcentury America*, edited by Monica Obniski and Darrin Alfred (New Haven: Yale University Press, 2018).

## DISCUSSION POINTS

- Where do design and jazz intersect?

- Improvisation is important in graphic design. But how important?

- What comes first, a design strategy or improvisation?

- Is abstraction more playful than systematic?

*Nineteen eighty-four was an auspicious year. George Orwell's 1948 book,* Nineteen Eighty-Four, *introduced Big Brother; in an Orwellian 1984 TV commercial, Apple introduced the Macintosh computer. In 1984 Emigre Graphics / Emigre Fonts published the first issue of its rule-bashing typography magazine,* Emigre, *the clarion of the new graphic design.* Emigre *forever changed graphic design. After three decades, Rudy VanderLans and Zuzana Licko, the husband and wife team that founded Emigre and designed or promoted many of the emblematic digital fonts used on computers and in print then and now, have not rested on their laurels. While they continue refining old faces and conceiving new ones, the trailblazing is over. A few years ago I had an opportunity to ask VanderLans to recall the early days of digital typography.*

# The Emigre Font Legacy

"Most designers were telling us the Macintosh was a fad without any use for serious graphic design," he says about the early years. "So at the time we felt very isolated within the design community. We weren't taken seriously at all. We enjoyed the challenge and opportunities this tool offered, but we had no idea how big it would become and that it would solidify our place within it."

*Emigre* magazine, each issue of which was designed in a radically different style from the last, some by guest designers, introduced a fanatical new generation of designers to alternative ways of making typography using the Mac, which drove the older, rational modernist generation nuts. But then in 2005 the magazine ceased publishing, in large part because of the tremendous expense, financed by type sales, that declined when the economy dipped. But there were other reasons to discontinue *Emigre*, VanderLans says. "The world of graphic design was changing, the focus became the internet and blogs, and I felt disconnected from much of it. It was too geeky for me."

Although some of the articles and many of the letters to *Emigre* would later influence certain design blogs, VanderLans felt "the design conversations online were all very instant, and short, like snapshots. I like long, drawn-out essays. I like to think about things. I need time to reflect. So I lost my appetite for design discourse and started focusing entirely on our typefaces and the design of our type specimens."

Emigre Fonts once included eccentric novelty display types, but at the point in the mid-2000s "when everybody seemed to have caught the type design bug, there was such a glut of novelty fonts being released, we realized we had to focus elsewhere," VanderLans notes. "It was also a part of growing up. We wanted to continue to challenge ourselves in our work. Designing text fonts [as opposed to headline or title fonts] requires a different set of skills. It also required a different type of specimen booklets to be designed, far more systematic and rational, and far less expressive."

The most popular Emigre font is Mrs Eaves (and Mr Eaves), a continually expanding family of faces, now including the recent release of Mr Eaves XL Sans and Modern Narrow. The marketplace seems to demand new faces, yet VanderLans says, "We always like to think we're independent from the marketplace, it's the artist in us. But when our customers drop hints about what they would like to see, we listen. Mrs Eaves became very popular, and people started to ask for additional weights and variations. Zuzana was always interested in exploring the idea of creating a sans serif based on the structure of Mrs Eaves serif. So she spent the past three years drawing variations on Mrs Eaves, resulting in a family of ninety-six related fonts, including sixteen serif styles and eighty sans styles."

The reason for so many variations is that the original Mrs Eaves is not a typical reading face. (For the type nerds reading this, here's VanderLans's rationale: "It's spaced a little too loosely for lengthy texts and the x-height is too small. And although I've seen it used in books, it works best in shorter texts when there is room to set it bigger with ample line spacing. It also works really well in poetry. And we've seen it adorn hundreds of book covers. It's the additions, Mrs Eaves XL, where we increased the x-height and tightened the spacing, and the companion Mr Eaves XL Sans fonts, that can easily compete with some of the best text fonts out there.")

Although VanderLans steers clear of social media, he and Licko have adapted many of their designs for web use since the iPad and handhelds are the platforms of the day. Their brand-new face, called Program, currently in development, is what VanderLans calls "a type designer's typeface. It's very much about typeface design and the challenges that type designers encounter when they design type." (Again, for the type aficionado: "It features both rounded edges evoking the effects of reproduction, and ink traps, the technique used to counteract the effects of reproduction. It also mixes different stem endings, structures, and weight distributions in a way not usually done in a family of fonts. The idea is to create a series of fonts with strong individualistic features, almost busting the constraints of a central theme that is usually imposed on a family of fonts, while still relating to each other in terms of overall look and feel.")

When Emigre started, there were only a handful of digital foundries. Now, with the internet, there are literally hundreds of websites selling hundreds of thousands of fonts. It's become extremely competitive. "One way we hope to set ourselves apart is with our promotional material," VanderLans says, referring to the aforementioned specimen sheets. "We're one of the few type foundries left that still publishes printed type specimens . . . because it is a big expense. But since most typefaces are still designed primarily for use in print, it only makes sense to send people printed samples of the typefaces."

Yet VanderLans admits he is still very impressed, "jealous even," by all the incredible typefaces that are being produced by young designers these days. "When I look at the work that comes out of the colleges KABK in The Hague and Reading in the UK, I'm just amazed," he says. "These young design students spent only a single school year studying type design and they finish with fully formed, professional-looking type designs. But I am also struck by how conservative most of the work is. You're young only once, and that's a great opportunity to experiment, to do something out of the ordinary. It's the one time in life that you can claim innocence and get away with anything and in the process perhaps create something emblematic."

Referring to the hoopla of the so-called design-culture wars of the 1990s, in which he and Licko played a role, over legibility and illegibility, classical versus experimental, VanderLans concludes, "I don't see any kind of larger conversation going on at the moment. There's no hoopla. [Type designer] Jeffery Keedy once mentioned that that period during the '90s was an aberration in graphic design. That it will likely not happen again. And the way that influences our work today is that we're feeling much more isolated again. Our type designs often responded to the larger conversations that were circulating around design in general. Now our work is far more inward looking."

---

Adapted from this article's original publication as "Can the Rule-Breaking Font Designers of Three Decades Ago Still Break the Rules?" in *The Atlantic*, November 8, 2012.

## DISCUSSION POINTS

- What are the technologies that have had the most impact on type and typography?

- Does new technology always dictate new ways of working?

- Will digital type continue to transform and/or mutate?

- Have you designed digital type fonts?

*Predictions of the death of print in the mid-1980s may have been dire, but they were also premature. Rather than signal the demise of an over 500-year printing legacy, the development of digital type technology helped resuscitate the field rather than send it to the grave.*

# Ray Gun and Apoplexy

Apple aired a TV commercial in 1984, claiming that the new Macintosh computer would make graphic designers obsolete because anyone could make layouts on their desktop. Yet that same year, the debut of *Emigre* magazine, the clarion of digital graphic and typographic design, proved that designers were not doomed but rather were shifting into another gear. There was more shifting in 1992 when an upstart music magazine called *Ray Gun* entered the digital vanguard, beginning its eight-year run until 2000. In the time-space continuum, this was, of course, a millisecond; yet in terms of publishing life spans, both magazines demonstrated that print media was thriving and moving in wild new directions.

Designer Neville Brody famously announced that both *Ray Gun* and the work of its founding designer, David Carson, indicated "the end of print," but of course *Ray Gun* was not the last bastion of print—far from it. In the early 1990s, it was the harbinger of an unprecedented typographic style-cum-language that challenged the status quo by engaging the computer on its own terms and treating it as an art form. The magazine was arguably as media-altering as the introduction of radio and television in their day, which print also survived.

But Carson was a "disruptor." He transgressed against the minimalist credo of mid-century modernism that was born in the Bauhaus and imported through Switzerland to corporate America; he challenged the geometric precision of the Macintosh and those clean, expressionless layouts promised in that 1984 Apple advertisement. Rather than follow a grid or template, Carson, who bragged about being self-educated in design and the new tools, employed many of the computer's early defaults to accomplish counterintuitive results that might best be considered anti-design. The *Ray Gun* designers who followed Carson, including Robert Hales and especially Chris Ashworth, only widened the schism, if anything, and proved a significant break had occurred within graphic design.

There had been forms of anti-design dating all the way back to the invention of graphic design in the late nineteenth century, when it emerged as a separate discipline within the printing industry. Rather than the purposeful, radical, or artful breaking of conventions and strictures, this early disruption was less revolution than evolution, whereby erstwhile typographers and compositors played with the various materials at their disposal. While many printers "experimented" in a hit-or-miss way, a few actually created art from an undisciplined craft.

*Ray Gun* was not in any way primitive—it was full-color and offset printed; it was professionally edited, art directed, photographed, and illustrated— but the digital technology was in its early developmental stages, so the conventions that we understand today had not yet ossified. With the newly available software like Photoshop and Quark, anything was possible. As a vehicle for graphic design, the magazine was a tabula rasa on various levels.

Focusing on trends in new music, *Ray Gun* had license to go where no magazine had gone before. Just as *Rolling Stone* established a standard for

*There had been forms of anti-design dating all the way back to the invention of graphic design in the late nineteenth century, when it emerged as a separate discipline within the printing industry.*

how "underground" or "progressive" rock would be presented in periodicals of the late 1960s, *Ray Gun* shrugged off the strictures that came before. Founder Marvin Scott Jarrett, founding editor Neil Feineman (who did the first two issues), and longtime editor Randy Bookasta may not have envisioned the aesthetic outcome, but they gave Carson, who had honed his eclectic typographic methods in the earlier niche *Beach Culture* magazine, considerable leeway in defining the magazine's overall graphic gestalt.

When Carson's *Ray Gun* premiered in 1992, *Emigre* was energetically promoting fonts produced by and for their digital foundry as well as the generation of graphic designers using them. These designers were also militantly attacking the old-guard designers for perpetuating a status quo, many of whom steadfastly defended the mid-century modernist traditions of rationalism and minimalism. Some of the old guard became outspoken critics of what was classified as grunge, new wave, or new New Typography. In other words, a minor design culture war predictably broke out between young and old. It was predictable for the usual reasons of one generation rejecting another and, more importantly, one technology being supplanted by another. If not for the transition from phototype to digital type, the battle would probably have been relatively mild. But there was a perfect storm brewing, with design organizations, exhibitions, and publications critically addressing one side over the other, and vocal loyalists on both sides of the design schism speaking their minds in design schools and in design institutions throughout the world. The 1990s was, in fact, exceptional for what was labeled "the new design discourse."

*The modernists were appalled by the irresponsible laissez-faire attitudes regarding essential design details, such as leading, word spacing, kerning, and line length.*

*Emigre* fomented discourse simply by publishing the work of experimental practitioners. *Ray Gun*, which earned significant publicity, polarized the opposing sides. The argument came down to legibility versus illegibility, and readability versus unreadability. But it touched another raw nerve. The more outspoken modernists carried the scars of earlier aesthetic battles. While blood was not spilled, the older generation—led in large part by dedicated designers and teachers Paul Rand and Massimo Vignelli—believed that their approaches to minimalism and precision were right, while complexity or anarchy was wrong. They felt that rational thought was better than thoughtless commercial art.

Although this older generation was probably not reading Carson's *Ray Gun*—and it was not designed for them in any case—nonetheless they saw his work and the wave of design he influenced in exhibitions, annuals, and magazines. The modernists were appalled by the irresponsible laissez-faire attitudes regarding essential design details, such as leading, word spacing, kerning, and line length. The rules that established graphic design as a prestigious field were being flouted in the names of fashion and style. Or so it seemed.

Paradoxically, many of the older generation venerated the earlier avant-garde movements, including Futurism, Constructivism, De Stijl, and others that vehemently fought the traditionalists and, in turn, took rampant liberties with type and image composition. While this internal criticism was flying, the general public was more or less oblivious to the war.

The average reader was little concerned about typographic design. *Ray Gun* appealed to its audience of music and pop-culture fans because it was not staid or conventional. Carson's typography may have been difficult to decipher, but the reader learned to navigate. Some *Ray Gun* writers and editors were disturbed when Carson created compositional roadblocks, but they understood to some extent that this gave the magazine its panache.

When Carson abruptly left the magazine in 1995, Jarrett's commitment to radical beauty presented a challenge to a new generation of designers. Young UK designer Robert Hales was brought in at the suggestion of graphics legend Malcolm Garrett at AMXdigital and immediately shifted *Ray Gun* away from the busy-ness of Carson's style. In 1997, Chris Ashworth and Amanda Sissons of the design team Substance took over the magazine after doing six issues of the company's title with MTV Europe, *Blah Blah Blah*. They brought with them a look that many still associate with *Ray Gun*: a take on Swiss typography that left it shattered and decayed—what Ashworth called "Swiss grit." It was no more legible than Carson's approach, but it had a most definite postindustrial look, as best defined by the covers featuring Bjork, Oasis, and Radiohead, which are some of *Ray Gun*'s most notable and reestablished the magazine as a design leader.

The proof was in the imitating. Dozens of indie mags and lookalikes followed *Ray Gun*'s lead. The anarchic, distressed, typographic gyrations— insulting to the fine-type masters of the past—symbolized a new aesthetic that belonged to the present. Younger designers took ownership of their codes.

*Ray Gun*'s chief attributes went counter to standard tenets of magazine publishing. The magazine's logo changed from issue to issue, and they ran coverlines that defied quick comprehension. The magazine did not follow a strict format or grid. Everything was reinvented each issue, although that in itself became indicative of a recurring format. Its direct competitors, *Rolling Stone* and *Spin*, had become more or less predictable, so unpredictability was its primary asset.

This unpredictability also became a reason for *Ray Gun*'s demise. Unconventionality has limits. *Ray Gun* is historically important today because it represents the triumph of counterintuitive "branding"—a moment before digital publishing turned from print to screen and magazines became increasingly more routinized. It also addresses the limitations of continual change as a viable strategy. Carson had to consistently raise the alternative design bar higher and higher, a Herculean task for any creative person or group. Even by the end of *Emigre's* long run, the magazine jettisoned its experimental stance in favor of elegant quietude—indeed a more standardized format—focusing more on text than typographical pyrotechnics. *Ray Gun* went down swinging.

Carson went on to apply his signature method to other magazines: *Speak*, which addressed popular culture more broadly, and *Blue*, which focused on Gen X travel. They were both interesting, even if less successful. Ashworth went on to become a creative director at Microsoft. But it is the freeform and chaotic energy of *Ray Gun*—what one of *Ray Gun*'s harshest critics, Massimo Vignelli, called "painting with type"—that deserves a prominent place in the pantheon of late twentieth-century magazines and digital-design history. It earned this notoriety by calling attention to exciting ways of playing with and being unruly with type, causing so much apoplexy among the establishment in the process.

Originally published in *Ray Gun: The Bible of Music and Style*, edited by Marvin Scott Jarrett (New York: Rizzoli International Publications, 2019).

# DISCUSSION POINTS

- Are magazines still influential media for graphic design invention?
- What is important about *Ray Gun* as regards the practice of contemporary type design and typography?
- What is the distinction between readability and legibility?
- How has type designed changed in an era when programs allow anyone to design type?

# Noticing the Public Notice

The public notice was carved, engraved, printed, and posted in public space to convey commands, proclamations, decrees, and warnings to all. What distinguishes it from its direct ancestor, the advertising poster, is that, as a rule (and tradition), the power of the public notice derives from the printed word rather than image. "[A]t the very heart of the phenomenon of writing . . . the study of the printed notice begins," writes Maurice Rickards in his classic *The Public Notice: An Illustrated History* (1973). He adds that the public notice was devised for another significant purpose: as an expression of intense social forces. "Its origins are close to the origins of law, order, government and hierarchy of power." So the public notice is not simply a throwaway trifle or trivial bit of paper, and, as Rickards asserts, these posted missives represent the exercise of overarching power of a monarch. "Historically, [the public notice] represents an extension of the power of the ruler—authority mass-produced."

Prior to the printed word, royal edicts and commands were broadcast through shouting chains of soldiers. In antiquity, athletes, notably marathon

*Whereas the poster offers the bright side of communications, the public notice was fairly grim. In general, they were typographically functional, without flourish.*

runners, also served as transmitters (Rickards notes that some dropped dead from exhaustion on completion of their mission). Thank heavens for printing. Yet when technology allowed for the production of mass-produced notices, widespread illiteracy among the masses required that a town crier read the notice aloud before it was posted, often accompanied by drum rolls or trumpet fanfares.

The public notice was a ruler's way of impressing his subjects and pressing virtual flesh. "[T]he document came to be seen as a tangible contact with the very will and person of the ruler himself," Rickards wrote. It was the most tangible means of exercising authority. Its posting was considered law, its desecration a criminal act. In the seventeenth and eighteenth centuries, the public notice was as much a weapon as a tool. It was also the origin of what George Orwell called Newspeak and what Rickards called "the resounding language of the throne room," which often began with "Whereas . . ." and quickly became the start of the legalistic jargon that continues to befuddle us to this day. With jargon came increased use of verbiage and the public notice's "fulsome sense of its own justification."

Another distinction from the traditional advertising poster is the somber essence of the public notice. Whereas the poster offers the bright side of communications, the public notice was fairly grim. In general, they were typographically functional, without flourish. Although type styles changed slightly in accordance with the spirit of the message, by contemporary standards, the multiple typefaces on some have an appealing retro-allure. Yet in their day, stern warnings were set with heavy gothic letters, quite different from calls for volunteers, where the tone of the "ask" required a lighter or friendlier typeface.

Today, the antique public notice is recognized for the hybrid fat faces— extra bold wood and metal types developed in the mid-nineteenth century by Robert Thorne and William Thorogood. There was such a flood of these impactful font styles, it seemed that an infinite number of them were at the printer's disposal. Rickards noted that these fat faces were the biggest thing to hit the printing industry in three hundred years because it was so quick in spreading throughout Europe and America too. "Printers who had been sedately chugging along with their book-style layouts suddenly found a whole new typographic world."

Perhaps the most important takeaway from this typographic explosion was how printers became content managers. Remember, there was no such thing as graphic design in the mid- to late-nineteenth century, so the printer was not just the layout expert but an editorial one too. It may have started with the modest printer selecting words that were typeset with bold or italic type for emphasis. Of course, the size of printing offered some real limitations, but as printers saw samples of more ambitious public notices, increasing numbers tried their hand at creating expressive type selections.

The standard look of a public notice evolved from simple type composition to more elaborate word-only concoctions. "In the ideal form the public notice stresses key words and phrases so as to convey an immediate telegraphic impact," Rickards wrote. To aid in creating the big bang, subsidiary clauses and qualifying phrases were usually set in smaller type.

Wanted posters, one of the most common uses for public notices in the United States and England, are perhaps the most fascinating for two reasons: the state of violent crime in the late nineteenth century, and the way the criminals were described. The most famous American poster of the genre is the "$100,000 REWARD!" for "THE MURDERER of our late beloved President ABRAHAM LINCOLN IS STILL AT LARGE." The typographic style of this and similar notices doubtless influenced the eventual screaming headlines in the tabloid newspaper format, developed in the early twentieth century.

The public notice evolved into the advertising poster in one direction, but continued pretty much as it was on into the present day in another. More efficient ways of distributing public messages developed—one of which was the public notices in most newspapers that in many places are required by law to announce land sales or local legislation—but there continues to be a need for certain written (text only) announcements, like life-saving warnings (i.e. the choking poster). What's more, today's notices do not use the same idiomatic and cropped language. Progress is inevitable, but how can current notice text beat the poetics of "PLEASE DO NOT SPIT IN THE CARRIAGES. IT IS OFFENSIVE TO OTHER PASSENGERS AND IS STATED BY THE MEDICAL PROFESSION TO BE A SOURCE OF SERIOUS DISEASE."

Originally published in *Print* magazine, Fall 2015.

## DISCUSSION POINTS

- What was the reason for posting public notices?
- Was typography an important consideration?
- Can a public notice be effective without good typography?
- Are public notices still relevant in the digital age?

*Signs bearing the words BEWARE, KEEP OUT, STOP, and CAUTION can readily be traced back to stone inscriptions in ancient Rome and mosaics in Pompeii, and even earlier in other civilizations. Warnings are some of the oldest and most common elements in the history of what is now called signage. They were meant to protect property and people from harming others or being harmed, as in accidentally falling off a cliff, drinking tainted water, or killing a neighbor's livestock. Here we examine the visual manifestations of cautionary declarations.*

# Signs of All Times

The earliest warning signs were not even 2-D signs, but rather symbolic and representational 3-D objects—bones, skulls, and sticks and stones lying on the ground or hanging from trees. With the coming of automobiles in the early 1900s, there was an even more pressing need for sign systems. In Europe, the most common of these were four pictorial symbols, indicating "bump," "curve," "intersection," and "railroad crossing"—each a recurrent danger. Traffic lights came later.

*Warning signs speak to the fact that despite human beings' natural aversion to pain or death, we often walk right into dangerous situations without knowing it.*

Of course, not all warning signs were intended for motorists. Signs with skulls and lightning bolts indicating live wires were popular in the early twentieth century—and remain so today. In fact, almost anything emblazoned with a skull (or "death's head") indicates that when touched, stepped on, or swallowed, tragedy is a real possibility. It was important to be cautious in business, factory, and ultimately machine work for obvious logical and practical reasons, including an accident's impact on productivity.

Warning signs speak to the fact that despite human beings' natural aversion to pain or death, we often walk right into dangerous situations without knowing it. Of course, in the case of cigarettes, we know the risks a million times over and still smoke. Signs were meant to be idiot-proof, or at least read by idiots, so to make and read a sign demands certain level of common-sense literacy.

In ancient Rome it was clear that a crucifix signaled death for Christian zealots or other criminals against the Empire, but it took a few gruesome executions before people understood the message, and even then they followed their own path, regardless of the consequences. Crosses of various kinds have, of course, over time become signs of faith, but in some ways they are also symbols of caution.

In addition to signs made of wood, stone, and metal, fabric flags and banners effectively communicate graphic warnings, and from greater distances too. The most common danger sign is a red flag, yet how it is perceived derives from its context. During those carefree Middle Ages, it was an indication that a town, hamlet, or village was in the grips of the black plague, which nobody wanted to mess with. But it also warned that combat was in progress. In either situation, it was better to stay away.

Among the most frequently applied warnings, "No Trespassing" has a long history, and might just be the most emotionally charged. These warnings stem from the biggest fears that business and landowners can have, notably liability from owning private property. Signs have long been a necessity in establishing boundaries, and around the globe they play a role in legal issues surrounding private property and criminal trespassing. This signage also defines the limits of privacy, vandalism, and theft prevention. (In the good old days some signs even stated "Trespassers Will Be Shot on Sight." Who said signs have no power?)

Sign removal can be a legal offense, and some jurisdictions have also criminalized unauthorized possession of road signs. The removal of warning signs without permission has led to manslaughter charges, and street artists who have vandalized signs by adding or distorting warnings are considered scofflaws and may be charged with misdemeanors.

Warning signs are not just essential tools in the graphic design arsenal— they are legal documents too. A simple "Beware of Dog" sign limits the owner's liability if said canine bites or mauls an intruder. Now that's design at its most powerful.

---

Originally published in *Print* magazine, Summer 2017.

## DISCUSSION POINTS

- What makes a successful cautionary sign?
- Other than the conventional signs and symbols, are there alternatives?
- Are there creative ways to express caution? Or must the message be simple and clear?
- What do you think of when you see a skull and crossbones on a sign?

# All Greek to Me

In the realm of text, there is no shame in being a dummy, for dummying is an essential activity of the design process. "Dummying" or "Greeking" text—creating jabberwocky or unreadable words to demonstrate the look of typeset columns or headlines—has a long and significant role in printing since the years after Gutenberg changed the world. Moreover, the nonsense words Lorem Ipsum, the most frequently used Latin words in Greeking, have roots in a piece of classical Latin literature from 45 BC.

The website www.lipsum.com cites the standard usage created by some anonymous printer from the sixteenth century:

> Lorem ipsum dolor sit amet, consectetur adipiscing elit, sed do eiusmod tempor incididunt ut labore et dolore magna aliqua. Ut enim ad minim veniam, quis nostrud exercitation ullamco laboris nisi ut aliquip ex ea commodo consequat. Duis aute irure dolor in reprehenderit in voluptate velit esse cillum dolore eu fugiat nulla pariatur. Excepteur sint occaecat cupidatat non proident, sunt in culpa qui officia deserunt mollit anim id est laborum.

According the same website, it was a Virginia Latin professor, Richard McClintock, who looked up one of the obscure Latin words, *consectetur*, from a Lorem Ipsum passage, and discovered the source in classic literature from sections 1.10.32 and 1.10.33 of *De Finibus Bonorum et Malorum* (The Extremes of Good and Evil) by Cicero, written in 45 BC, a treatise on the theory of ethics that was very popular during the Renaissance. The first line of Lorem Ipsum, "Lorem ipsum dolor sit amet," comes from a line in section 1.10.32.

It is certainly something of a phenomenon that such an obscure text, used for such an arcane process as layout, has lasted so many centuries unchanged. Nonetheless, it does the job magnificently, making very clear that whatever appears using those jumbled letters in the first line is not actual text—unless you belong to a design studio who use Lorem Ipsum on its shingle. Setting Lorem Ipsum as a block or columns nicely re-creates the exact word distribution and look of Latin-based alphabetic languages without the distraction that real text might bring to a dummy layout proposal. It is so successful that in the 1960s Letraset issued transfer sheets of Lorem Ipsum copy, but often type houses would set their own repetitive paragraphs for dummying purposes.

Still, there are other ways to Greek a layout. Galleys from unused or published layouts are often substituted for live text—although this is potentially dangerous if the text consists of real sentences that may be mistaken for the final product. And depending on the level of quality the designer is hoping to achieve from a dummy, it is okay—albeit disorienting—to place upside-down text to serve as dummy type.

Seismic shifts in technology and style have changed the design and printing industries during the past hundred years. While we have smart everything, from phones to watches, it is heartening that dummying remains the same.

Originally published in *Print* magazine, Fall 2015.

# DISCUSSION POINTS

- What is the advantage of using dummy type?
- Is there a disadvantage to dummy type?
- Are there any alternative forms of Greeking?
- When doing a dummy layout, is it better to use Greek type or gray boxes to indicate type?

# Ralph Nader: Design Critic

Ralph Nader's 1965 book *Unsafe at Any Speed: The Designed-In Dangers of the American Automobile* convinced my father to install seat belts in our 1960 Oldsmobile, which saved his life when, on a business trip, he swerved off the highway at night and landed upside down. No seat belts, no Dad. So I've always had a fondness for Nader the pioneer consumer advocate, even when he ran for president in 2000 tallying up over two million votes, making him the spoiler that arguably helped George W. Bush and Dick Cheney get into office. I did not like the outcome, but Nader deserved respect. Recently, he's entered murkier territory.

On February 27, 2019, Ralph Nader posted a piece on Nader.org titled "Unleashed Graphic Designers: Art Over Function" in which he regurgitates many of the usual complaints about legibility since Gutenberg ("Hey Johannes, can you make the type larger and we'll have 32 instead of 42 lines so the older monks can read it more effortlessly?") This new article is laced with generalities and untruths about contemporary newspaper design.

"In today's print news, legible print is on a collision course with flights of fancy by graphic artists," his blistering attack begins.

"Admittedly, this is the golden age for graphic artists to show their creativity. Editors have convinced themselves that with readers' shorter attention spans and the younger generation's aversion to spending time with print publications," he argues cogently, "the graphic artists must be unleashed . . . Space, color, and type size are the domain of liberated gung-ho artists."

Yes, that's exactly what designers do—they balance space, color, and type size—as opposed, to say, operating the Hadron Collider.

"There is one additional problem with low expectations for print newsreaders," Nader hammers home. "Even though print readership is shrinking, there will be even fewer readers of print if they physically cannot read the printed word," he adds, without considering the reality that young people live on their phones (maybe that should be the target of his ire—unsafe at 5G). But Nader's not ignorant. He has to know that reading habits change from generation to generation, as do printing technologies. I guess he forgot.

"I have tried, to no avail, to speak with graphic design editors of some leading newspapers about three pronounced trends that are obscuring content," he notes. "First is the use of background colors that seriously blur the visibility of the text on the page. Second is print size, which is often so small and light that even readers with good eyesight would need the assistance of a magnifying glass. Third is that graphic designers have been given far too much space to replace content already squeezed by space limitations." All are reasonable concerns if news art departments were indeed guilty of doing this. Although some papers may be poorly designed, this is not the state of the field, the intent of most designers, or the reason that the industry is now faltering.

"Function should not follow art," Nader says, which is true, but show me where these problems occur in any major newspaper section and I'll vote for Mr. Nader the next time he runs for office. "Readers should not have to squint to make out the text on the page. Some readers might even abandon an article because of its illegible text! One wonders why editors have ceded control of the readability of their publications to graphic designers," he adds, referring to no particular designers, art directors, or editors that I've ever met. Editors are very turf-conscious. While Mr. Nader correctly states that "Editors cannot escape responsibility by saying that the graphic designers know best," I don't recall anyone like that among the many editors I've known.

"I am not taking to task the artists who combine attention-getting graphics with conveyance of substantive content. A good graphic provides emotional readiness for the words that follow." Thank you! But?

"However, in the February 17, 2019 Sunday edition of the *New York Times*, the page one article of the *Sunday Review Section* was titled, 'Time to Panic,' about global climate disruption by David Wallace-Wells. . . . The editors wanted to strike fear in readers to jolt their attentiveness to such peril, through a lurid two giant fingers with a human eye in between. A dubious attempt. Taking up the entire first page of the precious *Sunday Review* section (except for a hefty slice of an ad for the Broadway play 'To Kill a Mockingbird'), smattered by three paragraphs of small, white and almost unreadable text on a dark pink background, is counterproductive. Less graphic license and clearer type would have had art following function." Sorry, Mr. Nader, that was not "graphic license," rather eye-catching graphic design that, in fact, captured the audience's attention to read the story. Would another article have added more value to the readers? The art helped the function—and the function was to convey the story.

"Many graphic artists seem to have lost their sense of proportion—unless that is, the editors are pushing them to bleed out more and more valuable space with their increasingly extravagant designs," continues Nader's rant, ignoring the actual issues that drive news hierarchy. *The Sunday Review* is not a breaking-news section but a weekly review of critique, a magazine of sorts that "plays" a lead story based on its relative importance. Headline, photograph, or illustration are the tools used to signal that importance. "It is

> *"Many graphic artists seem to have lost their sense of proportion—unless that is, the editors are pushing them to bleed out more and more valuable space with their increasingly extravagant designs."*

bad enough that print publications have been shrinking due to diminished ad revenue. It is time for better editorial judgment and artistic restraint." "Artistic restraint" may be a good slogan, but it is bad practice.

"Unfortunately, there is no sign of such prudence. In that same Sunday edition of the *Times*, over *eighty percent* of page one of the *Business Section* was devoted entirely to a graphic of a presumed taxpayer smothered by flying sheets of the federal tax return—it rendered the page devoid of content." This illustration enhanced the story and triggered interest. "At the bottom of this front page, there was a listing of five articles under the title 'Your Taxes 2019.' I can only imagine *Times* reporters gnashing their teeth about having their prose jettisoned from being featured on this valuable page of the *Business Section*." What Mr. Nader calls "jettisoned" is a misstatement. Instead, front page referrals (or "refers") often result in more readers drawn into a section and tease even more stories. "That wasn't all. The artists ran amok on the inside pages with their pointless artistry taking up over half of the next three pages of this section," he says, presuming that articles on other pressing business topics never reached the readers. "Gretchen Morgenson's prize-winning weekly column exposing corporate wrongdoing used to be on page one of the *Business Section*. She is now at the *Wall Street Journal*." A pity for the *Times*, but it is not the fault of the graphics.

"This is happening in, arguably, the most serious newspaper in America—one that tries to adjust its print editions to an Internet age that, it believes, threatens the very existence of print's superiority for conversation, impact and longevity for readers, scholars, and posterity alike," Nader claims, yet

*Many graphic designers don't like to explain themselves or be questioned by readers.*

he has not come close to proving that the current *Times* is destroying print through its design. In fact, the contrary is true: new readers are coming to the paper version.

"I first came across run-a-muck graphic design at the turn of the century in *Wired Magazine*," he adds, turning his myopic eye to a pivotal magazine that was deliberately designed to be edgy and test the limits of print design and typography in the digital world. "Technology has dramatically reduced the cost of multi-colored printing. I could scarcely believe the unreadability and the hop-scotch snippets presented in obscure colors, and small print nestled in degrading visuals. At the time, I just shrugged it off and did not renew my subscription due to invincible unreadability." *Wired* was the first mass publication of the wired generation; Mr. Nader fails to recognize that it was expected to push boundaries of design in this early digital stage.

"Now, however, the imperialism of graphic designers *knows* few boundaries. Many graphic designers don't like to explain themselves or be questioned by readers. After all, to them readers have little understanding of the nuances of the visual arts and, besides, maybe they should see their optometrists," he crows. Although the "imperialism of graphic designers" has a clever sarcastic ring, it is, in fact, meaningless.

The last three paragraphs, however, prove that Mr. Nader has really gone off the rails since his folly of 2000: "Well, nearly a year ago, I wrote to Dr. Keith Carter, president of the *American Academy of Ophthalmology* and Dr. Christopher J. Quinn, president of the *American Optometric Association,* asking for their reactions (enclosing some examples of designer excess). I urged them to issue a public report suggesting guidelines with pertinent illustrations. After all, they are professionals who should be looking out for their clients' visual comfort. Who would know more?"

"Dr. Carter responded, sympathizing with my observations but throwing up his hands in modest despair about not being able to do anything about the plight of readers. I never heard from anybody at the Optometric Association."

"Of all the preventable conditions coursing across this tormented Earth, this is one we should be able to remedy. It is time to restore some level of visual sanity. Don't editors think print readers are an endangered species? One would think!"

Well, Mr. Nader, if you had critiqued graphic designers for illegibility crimes in the early 1990s, when digital typography was in its grunge and experimental phases, you might have had a reason for a modicum of outrage. But today it seems from this post that your once acute vision is sadly impaired.

_____

Originally published on *Design Observer*, March 13, 2019.

# DISCUSSION POINTS

- Is Ralph Nader correct in his critique?

- Does illustration often overpower text content in newspapers and magazines?

- Does it take a trained designer to be critical of design?

- Is the public perception of design more or less important than any other?

# THREE: POLITICS, IDEOLOGY, DESIGN

# Are There Limits to Free Speech?

I cannot speak to the legal intricacies of free speech guidelines, but I am an advocate of free speech principles. I believe that so-called acceptable speech changes as mores progress (or regress). Still, I am not an absolutist. I have biases that can (and do) sometimes override these principles. I cherish liberal interpretations of the rights of free speech. I also have strong ambivalences when some of those biases play out in real time. I guess we all do.

# *Freedom comes with certain subjective baggage and exacts a moral price.*

I oppose speech that puts others at risk. Language that agitates for violence and hatred cannot be tolerated; neither should talk or innuendo that libels and defames. Free speech should not abridge the rights of others to be free. However, this is not absolute. Freedom comes with certain subjective baggage and exacts a moral price.

So when I saw a poster protesting against extraditing Julian Assange to the United States, I had grave misgivings—not about hanging it, but about what it suggests. The idea behind WikiLeaks—to expose restricted information that the public nonetheless has a right to know, given the wont of government and corporations to keep secrets—is valid. Whistleblowers and leakers have done great service throughout history and many of them have suffered severe consequences for their bravery. But motive is a consideration when it is done to damage rather than to repair. Leaks must not simply expose wrongdoing but help legally remedy the wrong (if possible). I cannot help but question Assange's motives and reconsider my own support of his reasons for disruption. I support activist disruption when it serves my beliefs (admittedly, I am less of an advocate when it does not). Fighting against injustice is justified. But accepting free speech means understanding its ramifications.

This is where propaganda plays a role. The barrage of propaganda against Assange has raised serious doubts about his veracity. Is his activism for the right or the wrong reasons? Is he protected in the name of journalism or should he be investigated for political partisanship? The poster showing Assange with his mouth taped up makes it seem that America as a nation is against Assange, and that gives me pause. The gag is a clichéd graphic idea that has been used in many different iterations. Is the government trying to gag him? Yes. Do the people feel the same way? Not sure. But that's the responsibility of Americans to determine on their own and not take the propaganda at face value. George Orwell said that if free speech (or liberty) "means anything at all it means the right to tell people what they do not want to hear."

Free speech is not always righteous speech. Hitler was allowed to freely render his venomous rhetoric during the Weimar Republic, and then after it turned violent he was prohibited from public speaking by law. These rights were quickly reinstated by decree—look at how that all turned out. In times of war, information is closely guarded, so it requires strict classification— loose lips do indeed sink ships. Yet "Top Secret" should not be an excuse for unbridled censorship. Free speech is often used wrongly. That's the gamble. But then again, some speech should be proscribed. Remember we also have the right to remain silent—determining when is the big challenge.

---

Originally published as "To Free or Not to Free" on *Design Observer*, April 18, 2019.

## DISCUSSION POINTS

- What is free speech?
- What is free-speech absolutism?
- Can or should speech be banned when deemed harmful?
- What standards should be used for banning speech?

# Should a Designer Be Judged by Politics?

The Italian painter and illustrator Mario Sironi (1885–1961), a devoted Fascist, falls into a category that I refer to as "when bad things are done by good designers." Which begs the question: should Sironi's life be judged harshly for choosing to make art on the wrong side of history?

While in Rome a few years ago, I came across an extensive catalog for the exhibition *Mario Sironi and the illustrations for "Il Popolo d' Italia" 1921–1940*, curated by Fabio Benzi with the historical consultancy of Monica Cioli and the support of the Russo Gallery, which included 345 illustrations made by one of the greatest propagandists of twentieth-century Italian art for the official Fascist newspapers, magazines, and almanacs. I've known Sironi's work and have long been interested in the role of artists like him in dubious ideological activity. This caused me to ponder whether or not there should be a statute of limitations on those who made bad choices, ideologically speaking, yet were sincerely true to their convictions. With Fascism, its adherents were not simply dupes of a charismatic leader or populist rhetoric—arguably, through the benefit of hindsight, they aided in supporting a dictatorial state.

Sironi is a curious example of genius in the service of repression. A progressive artist who met the future Futurists Giacomo Balla, Umberto Boccioni, and Gino Severini when they were students at the Free School of Via Ripetta, Sironi practiced the "Divisionist" style, the art of separating color into individual dots or strokes of pigment. This formed the technical basis for neo-impressionism. In addition, he organized art salons that included Futurist founder F. T. Marinetti, while at the same time creating distinctive illustrations for *La Lettura* and *Gli Avenimenti* magazines that combined his personal approach with commercial art.

In 1913 he joined the Futurist movement, which Marinetti launched after publishing his 1909 "Futurist Manifesto." In 1914 Sironi took part in the *Esposizione libera futurista*, then engaged in pro-war activities with the Futurist group and signed the manifesto *L'orologlio italiano*. In 1919, Sironi's work was influenced by de Chirico's metaphysical art (representational yet incongruous imagery that influenced the surrealists in the 1920s). As with other personal influences, however, Sironi did not slavishly follow the pack but developed a language of his own.

In 1920 he was a signatory of the Futurist manifesto *Against all returns to painting*. In 1922 he jumped even deeper into the avant-garde, cofounding the group the Seven Painters of the Novecento, and joining forces with Margherita Sarfatti, an Italian journalist, art critic, patron, socialite, and

*This caused me to ponder whether or not there should be a statute of limitations on those who made bad choices, ideologically speaking, yet were sincerely true to their convictions.*

propaganda adviser of the National Fascist Party of Benito Mussolini. Although this group did not have a theoretical base, they followed Sarfatti, who introduced politics to this art. Sironi was the most unique of all the members, with his strong formal synthesis in combination with a rigorous spatial architectural construction.

While his painting developed, he continued as a ubiquitous illustrator. The Novecento group was presented at the XIV Venice Biennial; from this arose the idea of organizing a *Prima Mostra* of the Italian Novecento featuring art tied to Mussolini's rhetoric. It was inaugurated in 1926, in Milan, with the participation of 140 artists. Sironi designed the manifesto. In 1929 the *Seconda Mostra del Novecento Italiano* was inaugurated and was exhibited in Berlin, Paris, Barcelona, and elsewhere in Europe with Sironi as leader.

By 1931 Sironi was seeped in the passions of Fascism and produced, among other things, what might be described as Fascist/modernism. His fame as a painter and sculptor was growing, owing partly to his talent and partly his alliances with Fascists and Futurists.

In 1936 he received architectural and mural commissions, including the design for the Fiat pavilion at the Milan Fair. Yet it is through his illustration that Sironi was the leading interpreter of the Fascist ethos, "the new man," as one of the primary artists for *Il Popolo d'Italia* ("People of Italy"), a newspaper founded by Benito Mussolini, and a smartly illustrated color magazine, *La Rivista Illustrata del Popolo d'Italia*. Sironi made the Fascist image concrete.

# So is it fair to judge an artist by work produced during a particular era—a bad era?

*Il Popolo d'Italia* became the information organ of the National Fascist Party until Mussolini suspended publication. In his illustrations Sironi created characters and situations that characterized the Fascist era. With their biting satire he targeted political issues, opposing parties, the old liberal governmental class, the pro-democracy press, the democracies of America, France, and England, and, of course, Russian communism.

In the exhibition and catalog one sees one hundred works (selected from almost one thousand illustrations) created by one of the greatest exponents of Italian Fascist art. It's a double-edged view of an effective "political designer"—perhaps too effective. Whether for one side or the other, Sironi's aim was to propagate a political idea. Can he be condemned for supporting that idea? Or should his work, while viewed in the proper context, also be disconnected and viewed as art on its own terms? "In the illustrations for *Il Popolo d'Italia,*" wrote exhibition curator Fabio Benzi, "it hits the infinite variety of compositional and iconographic themes, never repeated but instead reinvented daily, with a wealth of visionary and symbolic depth, transfiguring reality but deeply rooted in it; so as to constitute an absolutely unique *unicum* in the history of illustration," adding that "political passion is inseparable from the artistic and aesthetics." So how should he be considered by history and posterity?

"Sironi's profound participation in fascist ideas," concludes Benzi, "led him to sublimate them in a monumental, imperturbable, and unquestionable style, contributing to set up a propaganda model also used in very banal and corrective ways." That is one side of the coin. The other is that as an artist, Sironi was actually more than his content—similar, say, to Ezra Pound.

Sironi's work in total is, argues the curator, "meditation on man, which he represents in his most solemn or in any case more total sentiments: pensive, inspired, involved in the drama, perhaps desperate, but always reminiscent of his noble nature, aiming at the absolute." I remain skeptical.

Sironi's work from 1945 until his death in Milan in 1961 grew out of a sense of political disillusionment and profound existential pessimism. With age (and defeat) comes wisdom, I suspect. The postwar years were devoted to "a spiritualized expressionism" and corrective sensibility. During the 1950s he produced abstract works "born ideally from the elaboration of architectural friezes developed in the thirties, but now intended with an absolutely autonomous sense." So is it fair to judge an artist by work produced during a particular era—a bad era? While reviewing Sironi's work, I could not entirely separate the motivations from the execution, while at the same time I could appreciate the execution for the success of his goal and the inimitability of his art and craft. Therein lies the paradox.

---

Originally published as "Should a Designer Be Judged by Ideology?" on *Design Observer*, June 15, 2018.

# DISCUSSION POINTS

- Should artists reveal their strong political points of view?
- What should be the consequence of being "politically incorrect"?
- How much time should elapse before an artist or designer should be held to account for past beliefs?
- Is it ethical for artists to contribute to bad governance?

# When America Leaned Fascist

Huey Long, the populist governor of Louisiana, purportedly said that if fascism comes to America it will be draped in the American flag and called Americanism. Unlike the rise of Italian Fascism and German National Socialism, what is described as American Fascism was not a "revolution" marked in its initial stages by paramilitary-led street violence. Despite the emergence in the 1930s of the "Fascist Shirts" (referring to the black- and brown-shirt rowdies in Italy and Germany and the Silver Shirts and white-hooded KKK in the US), American Fascism was led by men in suits passing tough regulatory laws rather than wielding head-cracking leaden bludgeons. According to cultural historian Wolfgang Schivelbusch in his revealing book

*Three New Deals: Reflections on Roosevelt's America, Mussolini's Italy, and Hitler's Germany, 1933–1939,* the hero of American liberalism, President Franklin Delano Roosevelt, actually had more in common with Europe's Fascist leaders than not. His WPA even used graphic design in a manner that suggested authoritarian ideas.

The New Deal, Roosevelt's socioeconomic program designed to extract the United States from the abyss of the Great Depression, was a rejection of classic, free-market liberalism in favor of a strong corporate state that stressed the importance of order, discipline, and planning. As early as 1912, FDR praised a Prussian-German concept of governance, stating, "They passed beyond the liberty of the individual to do as he pleased with his own property and found it necessary to check this liberty for the benefit of the freedom of the whole people." In 1934, the progressive writer Roger Shaw described the New Deal as "Fascist means to gain liberal ends."

Fascism was not a dirty word or deed at the outset. FDR adviser Rexford Tugwell wrote that when Mussolini came to power in 1922 following the socioeconomic devastation of World War I, he had done "many of the things which seem to me necessary." Lorena Hickok, a close personal friend of the progressive humanist Eleanor Roosevelt, said that if Roosevelt were actually a dictator, "we might get somewhere," adding that if she were younger, she'd like to lead "the Fascist Movement in the United States." The official Nazi newspaper, *Volkischer Beobachter*, praised "Roosevelt's adoption of National Socialist strains of thought in his economic and social policies" and "the development toward an authoritarian state" based on the "demand that collective good be put before individual self-interest."

Deplorable as it sounds, especially to all those who were raised in the glow of New Deal liberal progressivism, even in the 1930s, political and media critics attacked Roosevelt and his National Recovery Administration (NRA), the governing agency of the early New Deal that sought to impose regulations on business and industry, as well as price and wage controls, decrying "The Fascist Principles [in Europe] are very similar to those we have been evolving here in America."

Propaganda for FDR's program was relentless. The government bombarded Americans with demands to join the NRA and ostracized those who refused to participate. In what Schivelbusch called a "war of symbols," the NRA logo, the "Blue Eagle," presumably sketched by NRA director Hugh S. Johnson and designed by AIGA medalist Charles Coiner (who was celebrated for his design in *Advertising Arts* magazine), a blue spread-winged eagle holding lightning bolts in one claw and a gear in another, echoed the Fascist and National Socialist symbols of the era. It was conspicuously used in the United States by businesses to show compliance with the NRA, whose modus operandi the Supreme Court later declared unconstitutional. Its motto "We Do Our Part" sounds innocent enough, but Schivelbusch argues it was code for businesses to avoid being targets of sanctioned boycotts (code because it was illegal for the government to order a boycott).

Graphic design was integral to these social-political interventions. The NRA, Fascist, and Nazi brands, while visually distinct, nonetheless had both strategic and aesthetic similarities. They served the same purpose, too: engage citizens and exclude the opposition. Displaying signs and flags or wearing badges and buttons meant one was either for or against. Nonetheless, in the US, dissent was tolerated to a point—in Germany and Italy, heaven help you. But the underlying message was conformity, or else.

---

Originally published on *Design Observer*, January 9, 2019.

## DISCUSSION POINTS

- How does a logo function in a political context?

- Can liberalism be misrepresented by graphic design?

- How important is political history in the study of design?

- What are the limits of unfettered visual or verbal expression?

- How are rights protected and civility maintained?

- What is the designer's responsibility in maintaining or curtailing free expression?

*This is adapted from a talk I gave at the Norman Rockwell Museum in Stockbridge, Massachusetts, "You Say You Want A Revolution," about how struggle, turmoil, and conflict of the 1960s influenced illustrators of the period. This may not seem to fit a Rockwellian stereotype, but it was a logical part of the museum's fiftieth-anniversary programming. It coincided with the expanded republication of the original 1960 autobiography* My Adventures as an Illustrator *(The Definitive Edition), by Norman Rockwell as told to Tom Rockwell and edited by Abigail Rockwell (Abbeville Press) and the exhibition Norman Rockwell: Private Moments for the Masses. The following is an adaptation of my introduction from that book, an homage to Rockwell's heartfelt commitment to civil rights in the United States.*

# Norman Rockwell's Radical Painting

Never in his wildest dreams—and he had many throughout his life—did Norman Percevel Rockwell imagine that he would become one of America's controversial artists. Sure, he dreamed of being popular, respected, and accepted into New York society, yet mostly he compulsively worked hard to be as exceptional an illustrator as those he admired, including Howard Pyle, Frederic Remington, and others of the late nineteenth-century "Golden Age of Illustration." These (mostly) male artists defined the styles and content of American "commercial," "applied," and "popular" art. Rockwell saw his role as illustrator was to illuminate and entertain—to capture in paint what an author wrote in words. As the *Saturday Evening Post*'s most prolific cover artist for over forty years, his aim was to paint a mythic spirit of America, not kick dust in the viewer's eye. Being controversial—politically or otherwise— was never ever considered.

The name Norman Rockwell was as American as apple pie; his paintings were elegant, elegiac, and rousing tableaux that could be enjoyed by the masses. His good-natured *Post* covers were as integral to America's self-image as the Stars and Stripes and the national anthem.

Rockwell was (and remains) synonymous with rock-ribbed patriotic American values; his collected work was an archetype of what NYU professor Richard Halpern calls an "American innocence," which, in turn, also served to get him crowned "the king of kitsch," according to art critic Clement Greenberg. Taken at face value—and given the expression-filled faces of the many American types that he employed as models to populate his populist canvases—Rockwell could be considered the most effective propagandist for the American Way, perhaps ever. But there was controversy in some paintings—if not on the surface, then below the glaze.

In the late 1920s and '30s, as his star was rising, Rockwell was not entirely set free from the chains of the mob. Just as he created his American types, so too was he stereotyped as a prisoner of his own success, and he had to be somewhat circumspect about what and how he painted. When he rendered a schoolteacher in presumably harsh light, he had to endure the acrimonious letters from many schoolteachers. His public did not want him to veer from their proscriptions.

*Rockwell could be considered the most effective propagandist for the American Way, perhaps ever.  But there was controversy in some paintings—if not on the surface, then below the glaze.*

On a few other occasions, having been criticized for not being "modern," he attempted to work a modern touch into his art. He failed. What the public saw was to a large extent what and who he was. Throughout the early to mid-twentieth century, Rockwell was the paradigm of American commercial art, if not also a counterpoint for some. By the 1960s, illustration had moved away from the tradition of painting with models, but most significant was a wave of "conceptual" illustrators who Robert Weaver, as one of the best, described as illustrating interior ideas rather than exterior vignettes. Illustration was becoming more surreal, impressionistic, and symbolic. By the early 1960s, a new generation supplanted Rockwell and his cliched imitators.

In 1964, however, a year after he ended his contact with the venerable and prosaic *Saturday Evening Post* (because Rockwell, in fact, wanted to do work with more political gravitas) he published a major work of the civil rights era, *The Problem We All Live With*, as a centerfold in the January 14, 1964 issue of *Look*. The magazine offered him a place for his growing social concerns, including civil rights and racial integration. Rockwell went against type and placed black Americans as sole protagonists, instead of as observers, part of group scenes, or in servile roles. He produced a memorable document of the civil rights era, depicting ten-year-old Ruby Nell Bridges, the first African American child to desegregate the all-white William Frantz Elementary School in Louisiana, shown protected by four US Marshal escorts (who were only seen from the shoulders down).

Despite an abiding faith in America's values (as evidenced by his illustration of President Franklin Roosevelt's "Four Freedoms"), he was not blind to the nation's flaws. Rather than a propagandist, he was a visual commentator; rather than subservient to a client—be it a product or a magazine—he was true to his conscience. He made hundreds of heartfelt portraits of America, but *The Problem We All Live With* is arguably his most socially vital work and is so resonant still.

---

Originally published as "Rockwell's Most Radical Painting" on *Design Observer*, August 2, 2019.

# DISCUSSION POINTS

- Rockwell's work for the *Saturday Evening Post* represented mainstream America— was it right for him to expect the magazine to publish an image like *The Problem We All Live With*?

- Was it heroic for Rockwell to be true to his conscience?

- How much influence did *The Problem We All Live With* have on the nation's understanding of racial equality?

- What is the most striking—powerful—aspect of this work?

# A Day
# Trip into
# Darkness

It is 3:13 on Monday morning in Krakow, Poland. It is dark out. I cannot sleep. In a little over five hours I will climb into a VW minivan with six strangers for the ninety-minute daytime drive to Oświęcim, the Polish town that the Nazis renamed Auschwitz, which together with neighboring Birkenau was the largest of all the Third Reich's hundreds of concentration camps.

Since childhood I have been obsessed with the Holocaust. I have seen films (fiction, faction, and documentary); read histories, articles, novels, biographies, and memoirs; visited museums and archives; attended memorials and services; and constructed a vivid diorama in my mind of the iconic and horrific scenes that define the mass extermination of Jews, Poles, Gypsies, and many others in the abomination that was the Holocaust, or Shoah. I never met the members of my grandmother's immediate family who were unlucky enough to be born and murdered at the wrong time and place in history. I have internalized a wide range of images that attest to the brutality they must have endured. I have assimilated and aggregated these visions in my imagination and suffered vicariously through their unimaginable ordeals. Yet despite this overwhelming—at times self-indulgent—fascination, I had never been to the actual source. Today is the day my internal images will become real—and imbued with new relevance.

Friends have said this will be cathartic, enlightening, sad, and traumatic. I liken it, somewhat, to an adopted child or adult meeting a birth parent for the first time. Maybe this is apt and maybe not, but for me the Holocaust has been like standing behind a one-way mirror. Now I'll walk through it.

Some people told me not to go; others, not knowing how to respond, told me to "enjoy" my trip. The wisest advice I received was to make some time to contemplate the experience and to be very careful not to overly (or disingenuously) identify too much with the victims. I am not a victim or even close.

Before leaving for Poland I explored (and asked others to help identify) genealogy websites to find—without any luck—what I could about my great-grandfather (on my mother's side), whom I honor with my Hebrew name. His name was Shmuel [Samuel] Zucherbrot [sugar bread, or sugar loaf]. I am Chaim Shmuel. My grandmother's father died along with my great-grandmother (whose name I never learned) and another daughter (an aunt also unknown to me) either in the Łódź Ghetto or in Auschwitz–Birkenau. Any chance I had to obtain additional family details died three decades ago along with my grandmother, who did not care to discuss the Holocaust at all, and who I stupidly never asked, despite my interest.

It is 3:45 now. It took around a half hour to write the above. I turn off the computer (set on dull light) but I cannot fall back to sleep. I cannot stop thinking about how I will ultimately feel when I see firsthand the famous iron Auschwitz gate topped with the mockingly sarcastic slogan "Arbiet Macht Frei" (work will make you free) and the indelible specter of the Birkenau portal through which passed hundreds of cattle cars filled with dead and dying souls. How will the concrete electrified fence poles, the barracks still standing after seventy-three years and foundations of those collapsed wooden ones, stretching in row upon row for acres, haunt me? I anxiously—indeed guiltily—ponder what it will be like to actually set foot in a parking lot adjacent to the largest death "camp" in the world for a three-hour look-see, and then return to Kraków for a delicious dinner with friends at a lovely restaurant serving foods that will remind me of my grandmother's cooking. We'll see.

It is 4:00 p.m. and I am back in my Kraków hotel room. The anticipated visit is over. Not a word was spoken by anyone on the way back. Only a radio station playing perky Polish pop dance music broke the silence.

The tour began with a young, blonde Polish guide. Her narration was bloodcurdling yet calming in its pleasantly accented delivery. I listened to her melodious voice amplified through a headset as she spoke into a clip-on microphone. Other tour groups with other guides passed by, but they were blurs. I listened to our guide's audible breathing as she spoke with compassionate authority about the people who suffered the unthinkable horrors presented in each of the two-story brick barracks (neatly arranged former Polish army housing) that was Auschwitz I. I spoke to no one, no one spoke to me—I had no wish to share my thoughts with others. I only looked at the evidence—the severe wooden stalls in which inmates slept on straw; the few seatless toilets that each person could use only twice a day for five minutes at a time (or face extreme punishment), despite the rampant dysentery that left their bodies dehydrated; the hundreds of empty Zyklon B cans opened but not discarded after use; massive mushes of tangled, matted cut hair that filled an entire room; stacks of worn shoes and piles of spectacles, among the possessions collected prior to death. The guide reminded us that each shoe, each eyeglass belonged to an unknown person who believed with all their heart that Auschwitz (at first a labor camp) and Birkenau (intended as a mass extermination factory) was the first installment of a Nazi resettlement policy.

I looked for the name Zucherbrot as I walked past the massive vitrines filled with leather suitcases (many belonging to the over 1,000,000 children murdered by the Nazis and their accomplices). "It was better to kill children," said the guide, with a hint of anger, speaking about the Nazi guards, "than serve on the front lines."

The guide also said the images inside the buildings comprising the Auschwitz "lager" spoke for volumes. You can read millions of pages of documentation and literature (and watch *Schindler's List* a hundred times), but confronting that physical manifestation burns into your consciousness forever. However, nothing I saw—even Block 11, known as the "death block" because that's where the Gestapo interrogated, starved, and tortured their prey in a basement warren of cells designed to dehumanize even the animals among us—could have prepared me for the coup de grâce: the actual death chamber and crematorium that is so well known that it seems as though it cannot be real. It is definitely real.

Only one of the industrial gas chamber/shower and crematoria was not destroyed—the one, explained our guide, just a few hundred yards from the Commandant's villa, which the Nazis used to precisely test the most efficient quantity of Zyklon B pellets necessary to kill the largest number in the least amount of time. Our guide added that the barracks were necessary not to imprison but to detain Germany's victims until they could be murdered and their bodies disposed. The underground dressing stalls that led into the gas chamber, with its rooftop opening for pouring in the pellets that at a certain temperature turned to lethal, strangulating gas, which was adjacent to four large bakers' ovens for immediate corpse disposal, is *the* quintessential picture I cannot erase. And that was the point of the visit itself. For all the images conceived and produced to protest man's inhumanity to man, I have never seen a graphic or photographic work (and there are some amazing ones) that will ever do what that visit to that hell could do.

But there is also some cognitive dissonance. Once supposedly secret, Auschwitz–Birkenau is a "destination." The very place that no sane person would ever want to be sent to is the very place, on this cold, overcast day in March that I visited, that hundreds of co-visitors felt the need to see for themselves. People of all ages, nationalities, and religions bought tickets from tourist agents in Kraków, stood in line to get their gratis receivers and headsets, and then afterward went to one of the three snack bars for sandwiches, sausages, and sodas.

I once heard about a survivor of the camp who, decades after the ordeal was over, at his daughter's dinner table, would roll up tiny wads of bread and place them in his pocket, just as he did when he was at Auschwitz. I thought of him as we were released to have snacks and drinks at the stands. I did not eat. Most of all I thought and thought and thought. I'm still thinking as I finish this around 3:00 a.m., not being able to sleep again.

---

Originally published on *Design Observer*, March 15, 2018.

# DISCUSSION POINTS

- How are designers complicit in the development of concentration camps?

- Are designers, engineers, and architects complicit through their work?

- Can Auschwitz forever be a deterrent from crimes?

- What purpose do monuments serve in society?

# My Dystopian Reading List

After the 2016 election I decided to relieve my frustration and despair by reading as much classic dystopia lit as possible. Regardless of the reality, fiction is fiction—an escape valve, so to speak—until it becomes real. The following is my reading list for people, like me, who can cope with the high anxiety these books will trigger. This is a partial list.

Now is a good opportunity to read Sinclair Lewis's 1935 bestselling novel *It Can't Happen Here,* in which a crafty demagogue, Democrat/populist senator Berzelius "Buzz" Windrip, takes the presidential nomination away from incumbent FDR and beats his Republican challenger. Upon taking office, Windrip outlaws dissent, jails political enemies in concentration camps, and recruits a paramilitary group of thugs called the Minute Men, who violently enforce the policies of the new "corporatist" state. The "Corpo" curtails women's and minority rights and eliminates individual states, subdividing the country into administrative sectors. When *It Can't Happen Here* was first published, America First, Christian Front, and German Bund organizations were rapidly growing around the country (including in New York City and Los Angeles), advocating revolution, with many members of Congress playing supporting roles. Despite the racist and nationalist rhetoric, this real threat to democracy wasn't allowed to happen here.

Lewis's ominous portrayal of fascism "coming to America" wrapped in the American flag was echoed in Philip Roth's 2004 *The Plot Against America*, wherein aviation celebrity Colonel Charles Lindbergh, a vocal supporter of Hitler, becomes the candidate of the America First Party, which opposes US intervention in World War II, accusing the "Jewish race" of trying to force war with Germany. This was indeed true. The story, which is fiction, begins with a landslide upset win for the presidency against FDR. Lindbergh immediately signs a treaty with the Nazis and the Japanese to not thwart their respective expansionist plans. *Plot* was based on an actual movement of radical Republicans who supported a Lindbergh run for high office. It also draws on the vocal support in the US for Hitler and Nazi Germany's policies. Fortunately, it never materialized—although it could just as easily have happened here if a strong liberal were not in office.

For what I thought might be a change of pace, I next read Thomas Rick's 2017 *Churchill and Orwell: The Fight for Freedom*, which compares the biographical and philosophical similarities in the struggle to save England from the internal enemy—the "appeasers" who sought to make peace with Hitler—and the resistance, valiantly led by Winston Churchill. Although the outcome is known, the struggle to keep England afloat while fighting a persistent fifth column of English and Americans (notably, the American

> *Regardless of the reality, fiction is fiction—an escape valve, so to speak—until it becomes real.*

ambassador to England, Joseph P. Kennedy) was a huge challenge. Had FDR not stuck to his beliefs, there is no telling what the consequences would be, but the Nazis were sitting on England's doorstep.

Orwell's struggle to meaningfully help the war effort obviously leads to his two most influential books: *Animal Farm*, a metaphor for communist autocracy, and *Nineteen Eighty-Four,* a dystopian worldview and cautionary tale of what could happen if vigilance against demagoguery fails not just in totalitarian countries but in democracies too. *Nineteen Eighty-Four* addresses many of today's concerns of truth versus untruth, language versus Newspeak, and how, as Orwell wrote, "One does not establish a dictatorship in order to safeguard a revolution; one makes the revolution in order to establish a dictatorship.... The object of power is power."

The year 1984 has generally become a metaphor for the absolute autocratic (in this case Stalinist) state. In fact, Orwell wrote it as a warning against a development which is taking place in the Western industrial countries too, especially now. "The basic question which Orwell raises," wrote Erich Fromm in the paperback afterword to *Nineteen Eighty-Four* "is whether there is any such thing as 'truth.' 'Reality,' so the ruling party holds, 'is not external. Reality exists in the human mind and nowhere else ... whatever the Party holds to be truth *is* truth.'" Substitute the word "leader" for "party" and the consequence is the same. Truth is not an absolute any longer. And that is dangerous.

After *Nineteen Eighty-Four* I read the other two classic dystopias: Aldous Huxley's *Brave New World* (1931) and Yevgeny Zamyatin's *We* (1921). Huxley's book predicts our drug-dependent/controlled society. It takes place in World State, in London in 2540 AD, where citizens are artificially raised in engineered wombs and through a childhood indoctrination program based on intelligence and labor. A process of sleep-learning maintains its citizens' peaceful lives, though its famous happiness-producing drug called *soma* maintains the rest. People live in glass apartment buildings and are carefully watched by the Bureau of Guardians.

*We*'s plot begins one thousand years after the novel's so-called One State's conquest of the entire world. The dystopian society depicted in *We* is presided over by the Benefactor and is surrounded by a giant Green Wall to separate the citizens from primitive untamed nature. All citizens are known as "numbers." Every hour in a citizen's life is directed by "The Table."

I had never heard of Jack London's *The Iron Heel* (1908). Generally considered to be "the earliest of the modern dystopian" fiction, it chronicles the rise of an oligarchic tyranny in the United States. Jack London's socialist views are most explicitly on display. The book is unusual among London's writings (and in the literature of the time in general) in having a first-person female protagonist written by a man. Much of the narrative is set in the Bay Area, including events in San Francisco and Sonoma County.

---

Originally published as "My Pre-Holiday Dystopia Reading List" on *Design Observer*, November 15, 2018.

## DISCUSSION POINTS

- What benefit is there for designers to read fiction?

- Is the mix of politics and design something to be addressed in design school?

- How can all points of view be heard and discussed?

- As policy, some schools prohibit the inclusion of political issues in the curriculum. What is the advantage or disadvantage of this?

*Founded in the late 2017, the Tolerance Project was launched as a traveling poster collection to celebrate and honor the starting point of all meaningful social discourse: tolerance. Free, flexible, and ever-expanding, the Tolerance Project brought a message of social acceptance to more than 100,000 people in twenty-four countries worldwide. Artists from each nation are asked only to illustrate the word "tolerance" in their native language. The posters appear in public spaces—in parks, on university campuses, even on buses—thus engaging with a wide cross-section of the population. It's all part of starting a conversation about inclusion, which can only begin with a foundation of tolerance—and spreading respect in a world increasingly split by race, religion, sexuality, and national origin. This essay addresses universal messages and personal visual language.*

# Tolerance: Spreading the Word

In 2017, Mirko Ilic, a Serbo-Croatian-born, New York-based designer and illustrator, did graphic design for the film component of the House of Tolerance Festival in Ljubljana, Slovenia, including an identity, logo, and posters, as part of a fundraising effort. After a year and half, to show appreciation for his work, the organizers offered Ilic a small square next to the festival with thirty poster spaces to show his work.

"I didn't think that it was appropriate to abuse my position and use this occasion to promote myself," he told me. So, in thinking about how to fill that space, he invited twenty-three internationally prominent artists, illustrators, and designers to create posters on the theme of tolerance. The only requirements were the size of the poster and that they had to write the word "tolerance" in their language and sign with their country of origin. "Less than four weeks later, I received all twenty-three posters." By 2019, the exhibit included 133 posters, with more on the way.

The problem with posters is ephemerality; one or two might over time have long-term impact, but most are buried under mounds of visual clutter. Ilic understands that no poster or any other creative activity can satisfy everyone. "If one walks through the Tolerance Poster show and if only one of the 133 posters that I have so far touches their heart, then the show has succeeded," he says.

The Ljubljana show was originally to be a one-off, yet seeing how beautiful and powerful the posters looked mounted in the square, "I became aware that only showing them there would be a huge waste of the talent," Ilic admits. What's more, the sense of the show's importance was reinforced the morning before it opened. Overnight, somebody destroyed one of the posters because it was in Arabic; a few days later, a few more posters were defaced. "It seems like certain people have a very strong reaction to tolerance," Ilic recalls. "This was proof of a lack of tolerance. But also a self-incentive to continue the show."

It is a novel model to keep adding to a traveling show. Ilic refreshes the offerings by inviting artists from the city where it is displayed. "People cannot invite themselves, although some do try," he says. There are two ways he goes about inviting people. "Whenever I am preparing for an upcoming show, I invite the most prominent or interesting artist or designer form the country where the show is to be held. That way I can have an artist with a local voice with local concerns with their own view on tolerance." Then, whenever he identifies an artist that could produce something new and interesting, they too are invited.

Drawing on his extensive Rolodex, having been art director of *Time* magazine's International Edition, the *New York Times* OpEd page, and

*But the strangest objection to the show happened in the United States—the title of the show.* Tolerance, *the exhibition committee insisted, was a negative title, and it made the show negative.*

organizing exhibits on other international themes, Ilic's core group included a United Nations of artists and designers: Hamzah Abdelal—United Arab Emirates; Reza Abedini—Iran; Tarek Atrissi—Lebanon; Peter Bankov—Russia; Michel Bouvet—France; Sue Coe—England/United States; Manuel Estrada—Spain; Milton Glaser—United States; Jianping He—China; Fons Hickmann—Germany; Anette Lenz—France; Mwalimu Saki Mafundikwa—Zimbabwe; Alejandro Magallanes—Mexico; Chaz Maviyane-Davies—Zimbabwe; New Collectivism—Slovenia; Istvan Orosz—Hungary; Paula Scher—United States; Yuko Shimizu—Japan; Sarp Sozdinler—Turkey; Felipe Taborda—Brazil; David Tartkover—Israel. Now there are 133 posters from seven continents and fifty-four exhibitions in 24 locations. Not everyone asked agreed, however, and a few wanted to be paid. No one is paid, and the venues that take the show (which is distributed as digital, downloadable high-resolution files on the internet) must find funds for making the physical artifacts and finding space to exhibit them.

In fact, a requirement of getting the show is that some, if not all, of the posters be shown in a public space where everyday people can see them. "I am always desperately trying to avoid galleries and the label of a design show because those kinds of shows mostly attract the usual suspects, people who already attended design shows and galleries," Ilic insists. Since most of the shows are in public places, every show is aimed toward the space and financial possibilities of whoever is hosting the exhibition. For the show in Konstantinovka, Ukraine, which was organized by local activists with no money, everything was printed on the only available printer that could print at tabloid size. In 2019 in Ljubljana, Slovenia, the same posters were printed billboard size (because the show at that time was sponsored by a billboard company). Also in 2019, the same posters appeared as a wrap on the Dubrovnik city transportation city buses, because the show was sponsored by the city of Dubrovnik, Croatia. "None of this can be planned ahead. The moment the show is agreed upon, the organizers look for the most effective way to display posters," Ilic says. Sometimes they are not only printed but also digitally projected, as in Salt Lake City, Utah; Dubrovnik, Croatia; and Jakarta, Indonesia.

It is not always smooth sailing. Censorship has occurred, and Ilic is reconciled to the problems. "There are many aspects of why people will have an objection," he explains. "Some are legitimate," including two posters in the show representing a swastika (Herms Fritz and Alex Jordan). There are a few countries in Europe that forbid the public display of even non-Nazi versions of the symbol. In some countries the public display of nudity, even when it is a statue (Leonardo Sonnoli, Jose Albergaria), is also illegal. "But, some things I cannot understand very easily," Ilic says. "I had a case where the potential exhibitor in Kuwait wanted to display only forty posters from the one hundred we had at the time because the other sixty were 'inappropriate.' They didn't want a poster with people dancing, because public dancing is illegal (Niklaus Troxler) or a poster with knives kissing, because it was 'too sexual' to show (Edel Rodriguez). Under those conditions, we could not have a show."

But the strangest objection to the show happened in the United States— the title of the show. *Tolerance*, the exhibition committee insisted, was a negative title, and it made the show negative. "I lost a grant opportunity from Sappi [Global's] 'Ideas that Matter' when a juror refused to give the project a grant . . . and suggested that the show needed to be called 'Inclusion' instead of 'Tolerance.' I received the same comment from multiple places—all *here* in the United States. Obviously we have some misunderstanding here." To date, no grants have been forthcoming.

And this is a major problem. *Tolerance* is an international show. In most countries around the world, people understand the meaning of the word "tolerance." Ilic insists the word "inclusion" does not reach a broad range of languages. In some of the countries where they had the show or wanted to have the show, even tolerance is a lot to ask. "Gay people get harassed and beat up, they could even be jailed. Females, for one reason or another, are constantly harassed. Not to mention the harassment that people of ethnic and religious minorities are going through. For most of them, tolerance is what they desire. We must first achieve tolerance to even talk about inclusion. By the way, even the United Nations declared November 16 as the International Day of Tolerance."

For the last two and half years, all of the preparation work for the Tolerance Poster show has been financed by Ilic alone. Most available grants cater to artists or to nonprofit organizations, so Ilic became a nonprofit: "Tolerance Project Inc." Ilic's goal is simple: use posters to raise awareness and grow the conversation. "If tolerance succeeds," he says, "I won't need to produce more shows around the world anymore. Then, maybe I need to work on shows of 'inclusion'?"

---

Originally published on *Design Observer*, October 4, 2019.

# DISCUSSION POINTS

- Can universal themes like tolerance or inclusion be addressed with a personal vocabulary?
- Has political correctness become an issue in making graphic design?
- How does one organize an advocacy or protest exhibition?
- What is the difference between advocacy and dissent?

*In just under two years, President Donald Trump has imploded many of our notions of liberal American democracy, turning this nation from a star of great magnitude into a black hole. We have become Bizarro World, where freedom is proscribed by anti-progressive leaders and retrograde policies. What was up is now down; what was impossible is now probable. "Make America Great Again" is a threat, not a promise. Tiki torches are symbols of hate, not givers of light. The lunatic fringe is no longer on the fringe, and the plot against America is gathering momentum. This essay for the exhibition "Art as Witness" addresses the possible curative power of political graphics.*

# Welcome to Bizarro Land

The current unfathomable twist of fate is not entirely the fault of the current president or his compliant Congress, although together they enable its perpetuation. Bizarro is historically a parallel Amerika, a muster of festering evil coalitions of white supremacy, religious intolerance, economic inequality, racial and gender inequity, and a slew of other prejudiced America-first nationalisms gathered under the big top of populist patriotism. Those who advocate today's Bizarro view of America have new names and young faces, but their fundamental dogma is as old as the Republic itself.

As a nation, America has intermittently experienced mass mood swings (a kind of national bipolar disorder). Challenged by battling economic, political, and religious forces and the demigods that emerge to champion them, American liberty routinely takes one step backward for every two steps forward. When the nation is on its meds, progressive legislation gets passed and change moves forward. Rights that did not exist in earlier times become law—women's right to vote, gays' right to marry, and the end of slavery among them. But when America goes off its medication, watch out! Demons emerge. Generations are ruined.

Living in the current Bizarro era feels different than other oppressive downturns. Rather than a temporary condition that will invariably be adjusted by election therapy, the rise of American illiberalism appears more palpably threatening than ever before.

The status quo has never been stable. A review of political and social graphic commentary over the course of this nation's history reveals that every generation since founding father Benjamin Franklin drew the first 1754 political cartoon "Join, or Die" has attacked some aspect—real and imagined—of perceived tyranny, injustice, and corruption. The only constant is that tyranny, injustice, and corruption existed side by side with democracy, freedom, and liberty and have kept each other in check. Americans have been fighting for and against right and wrong for over 250 years, switching sides as it suits their self-interest. For a quick course in American bipolar-ism, watch Steven Spielberg's *Lincoln*, which, against the backdrop of the Civil War between blue and gray, shows just how many shades of blue were also warring among themselves. Or go back to the nineteenth-century cartoons in *Harper's Weekly*, *Puck,* or *Judge* that vividly portrayed how American ideological factionalism almost (yet miraculously did not) destroy the nation.

Political graphics are not just records of ebbs and flows in American politics; they are integral documentation for mapping the timeline of the fragile American experiment. There is an assumption that visual commentary is always oppositional, although in fact the majority of it is by definition critical. Not all cartoonists, illustrators, and designers are a priori rebellious. Disapproving or dissenting graphics are more prevalent because contentment does not breed internal conflict; attacks or critical barbs at

> *Now is the time to produce statements that puncture holes large enough to let the carbon out of his bubble.*

issues or personalities produce decidedly more interesting satire. Still, those in power also manufacture propaganda that can be just as convincing for their entrenched conservative side. After the 2016 election, Trump supporters on the ultraright produced reams of graphic material—much of it very similar to the look of anti-Trump visuals—that rang true to his base.

It is not the intention of this exhibition, however, to show, contrast, or compare these two opposing camps (Trump has a big enough bully pulpit to exercise his bullying). We have come to bury the orange Caesar, not to praise him. This selection of images created since Trump became the dealmaker of the free world is meant to show the current status and scope of the visual opposition. This show exists for two reasons: to celebrate the high level of creative output in reaction to and cautioning against policies gnawing away at American freedoms, and to determine whether or not these images are indeed staving off the process of Trumpian normalization that is eroding American consciousness.

The biggest challenge for artists and designers in responding to Trump's growing autocracy is not to get so roiled that their personal disgust overpowers facts. Now is the time to produce statements that puncture holes large enough to let the carbon out of his bubble. Oppositional images cannot be indulgent— they must do some real perceptual damage and trigger change. Of course, images alone will not fix what's wrong—voting will. But many images, on many platforms, barraging the enemy at every turn with as much conceptual firepower as possible might make anti-Trumpists angrier and—perhaps— change the attitudes of those on the fence. Maybe!

The danger of such barrages is its normalization. It is easy to ignore the rants of those who draw (literally and figuratively) from common playbooks. We demand that the artists and designers who are fighting the battle do not just repeat the familiar canards and refrains. The best satire should not mimic the same slogans or images. Art against power is only as good as the heart-piercing impact it has on the viewer, and the most powerful of these capture feelings through the truth that gets visualized. Laughter is fine if it is an entry point or a call to action. One hopes that the polemical pictures selected for this exhibition will not just make "good clean fun" of the most dangerous presidential Bizarro in modern history, but will help expose it, strip it bare so that the emperor really has no clothes or anything else behind which he can hide.

---

Originally published in *The Master Series: Steve Brodner* (catalog) (New York: School of Visual Arts, 2019).

## DISCUSSION POINTS

- Can political cartooning and caricature change people's attitudes?
- What is the most effective aspect of political graphics?
- Can political graphic commentary take a middle-of-the-road position?
- Is partisanship endemic to political discourse?

# The Unsmiley Face

Every absolute ruler, monarch, prime minister, or president is entitled to an official portrait. It's a perk. Designed to capture authority, ubiquity, divinity— yet like the Wizard of Oz, there is flesh and blood behind the curtain. Sanctioned images usually reinforce the leader's omnipotence by obscuring any blemishes or flaws. When was the last time (or the first) that you saw an official portrait of a leader with sweat on his or her brow or with a five o'clock shadow or wearing glasses? Leaders hate wearing glasses (even Warby Parker frames). Queens look regal (not feminine), kings triumphant (not crazed from inbreeding), dictators strong (well, admittedly, Lenin looked rumpled), presidents often look like CEOs. This essay examines the political portrait, warts and all.

# When was the last time (or the first) that you saw an official portrait of a leader with sweat on his or her brow or with a five o'clock shadow or wearing glasses?

Official portraitists are never selected from the best of the best. They usually subsume their talents to the will of their subjects—and they have to be completely true to the subject's will (which means as stiff as possible). Last week one of the little-known masters of official portraiture died at eighty-eight. Wang Guodong was the Chinese artist responsible for the enormous portrait of Mao Zedong that looks over Tiananmen Square in Beijing in the way that Coca-Cola sign lights up Times Square (or the Camel man did decades ago).

Mr. Wang was chosen in 1964, when he was in his early thirties, to paint the fifteen-by-twenty-foot, three-story-high, metric-ton oil portrait of Mao that hangs steps from the party's central headquarters at the Gate of Heavenly Peace. Portraits of Mao have appeared there since 1949, when the Communists took power in China. Since they are exposed to the elements, the portraits are routinely swapped for fresher versions—so each year Wang Guodong repainted the exact same image (e.g., a painter's *Groundhog Day*).

Mr. Wang stepped down as official portraitist in 1976, yet his assistants continued to paint Mao as Mr. Wang designed him, showing the unsmiling Mao with his trademark chin mole. Other artists in other media—posters and textiles—gave Mao a bright smile, but since his teeth were black from neglect, some dental liberties were taken.

Wang is little known. Nobody is allowed to put their name on that painting. It is work for hire. And an honor. Anonymity was a duty. Unfortunately, Wang was not always honored. During the Cultural Revolution, from 1966 to 1976, Mao's image was prominently displayed by the millions and, as was the wont of the fanatical Red Guards, Wang was under attack by the student militants who persecuted anyone they considered ideologically impure or insufficiently devoted to Mao. Maybe it was the mole. In fact, his art directorial persecution was for painting Mao from an angle with only one visible ear. He was accused of implying that Mao only listened to a few people and not the general public. Wang argued that the painting was based on a photo issued by the government from which he was not allowed to deviate. He was still publicly humiliated by the Red Guard. He was rehabilitated, however, and Mao's ear was reinstated and listens to the people to this day.

Originally published on *Design Observer*, September 5, 2019.

## DISCUSSION POINTS

- What is the purpose of an official portrait?
- All such portraits capture artifice of its subject. Can you name a perfect portrait that is not stiff?
- Why are official portraits so heroic?

# Rebels with Cause: Ramparts and Scanlan's

In the 1960s, San Francisco's youth culture of acid rock, underground comix, radical lifestyle movements, and, not least, progressive counterculture journalism (including newsprint tabs like *Rolling Stone*, the *Berkeley Barb*, and the *San Francisco Oracle*) shocked and awed the world. Even more threatening to the established order, for their guile and grit, were two monthly magazines that went head to head with the status quo: *Ramparts* (1962–1975) and *Scanlan's* (1970–1971). Both challenged notions of "fair and balanced" journalism by reporting on what the mainstream dailies and weeklies were afraid to cover.

*The earliest issues were poorly designed, somewhat like a college literary magazine, with dreary illustrations and an undistinguished layout.*

Originally a liberal Catholic journal, *Ramparts* was founded by Edward Keating, a respected lawyer. The title referenced the national anthem lyric "the ramparts we watched." The earliest issues were poorly designed, somewhat like a college literary magazine, with dreary illustrations and an undistinguished layout. Keating was a reformer who simply wanted a vehicle with which to challenge conservative Catholicism. Nonetheless, *Ramparts* evolved into a fearless independent investigative magazine, uncovering government and corporate hypocrisies and promoting civil rights and social justice, while lashing out at communist witch hunters and CIA interventions at home and abroad.

*Ramparts* was considered the "soft left" until its renegade promotion director, Warren Hinckle II, and Howard Gossage, a San Francisco ad man with activist passions, pushed Keating into the shadows. Hinckle became *Ramparts*'s crusading editor-in-chief, and a ballsy investigative journalist named Robert Scheer was hired as the publication's investigative editor. Dugald Stermer (1936–2011), *Ramparts*'s art director from 1964 to 1970, once explained that he designed a deliberately restrained bookish format because it "lent more credibility to what must have seemed then like hysterical paranoid ravings of loonies." Hinckle never succumbed to partisan politics, but he uncompromisingly saw all sacred cows as moving targets. Scheer was skeptical of all isms and reported the earliest stories about CIA involvement in the Vietnam War.

The magazine published what would now be called underreported stories, including the confession of a Green Beret sergeant who, years before the *New York Times* published the Pentagon Papers, disclosed the US government's lies about Vietnam War policies. Stermer said *Ramparts*'s goal was to "raise hell," and among the magazine's bêtes noires was the hypocrisy of liberals who claimed to support social justice but nonetheless maintained a status quo relationship to power. *Ramparts*'s targets included Lyndon Johnson for the Vietnam War buildup, and Robert Kennedy, who was never forgiven for an earlier relationship with Senator Joseph McCarthy. *Ramparts* was a maverick that refused to blindly follow leftist dogma and never took anything—"not even their own side"—at face value, said Stermer.

*Scanlan's* was also a Hinckle brainchild. Hinckle was known as a tough intellectual hombre who wore a menacing black eye patch; he was a hard drinker, egotist, and publicity hound. He resigned as *Ramparts*'s editor and president on January 29, 1969, and the *Ramparts* board of directors declared bankruptcy soon after. To their surprise, however, Hinckle immediately announced that a new magazine, *Barricades*, would appear a month later, on February 25—though it actually took another year before it reached newsstands. With coeditor Sidney Zion, a savvy muckraker, Hinckle had struggled to find investors for the magazine, raising only $50,000 during that time frame.

Instead of looking for individual backers, they decided to raise the money through a public stock offering. The first day *Barricades*'s stock was issued, its price jumped from $3 to $4.50. In November 1969, the magazine's underwriter gave *Barricades*'s editors a check for $675,000. "Our deal with the underwriter was that the editors have absolute and dictatorial control of the magazine," they wrote in their initial manifesto. Their first act was to change the title to *Scanlan's* (purportedly after someone named John Scanlan, a pig farmer described by some IRA men that Zion and Hinckle met while touring Ireland as "the worst man who ever lived"). In late February 1970, the premiere issue showed the $675,000 check on its front cover, along with the editorial/manifesto printed large in Helvetica on the front and back covers.

*Scanlan's* was distinct from, yet editorially similar to, *Ramparts*. Both included investigative and muckraking journalism, literary criticism, film reviews, and photographic essays, but *Scanlan's* took no advertising in order to maintain its editorial independence. It did, however, run fake advertisements, like a parody for Lufthansa Airlines featuring a photograph of saluting Nazis with the slogan, "This year, think twice about Germany."

The first *Scanlan's* did not look at all like *Ramparts*, from its masthead to its typefaces. At *Ramparts*, Stermer used classical Times Roman and bookish formats. He relied on smart satiric illustrations from the likes of Ed Sorel, whose "Sorel's Bestiary" caricatured famous and infamous personalities as animals. Stermer also commissioned Seymour Chwast, Milton Glaser, Robert Grossman (who did one of his best Johnson caricatures for *Ramparts*), and Paul Davis, who executed a cover of South Vietnam's First Lady (technically, the president's sister-in-law) Madame Nhu in a cheerleader costume, for an investigative report into CIA recruitment of operatives in Vietnam. Stermer also hired Ben Shahn and Norman Rockwell and ran photomontages by Carl Fischer, who at the time was collaborating with George Lois on covers for *Esquire*.

*Scanlan's*, designed by San Francisco's supergraphics pioneer Barbara Stauffacher Solomon, was decidedly more modern-minimalist in the International or Swiss style—which is just what Hinckle wanted. Hinckle had known Solomon socially before he asked her to be art director of *Scanlan's*. Her friend June Oppen Degnan (sister of the poet George Oppen) introduced them. Degnan had also given Hinckle $25,000 to help start the magazine.

"Warren and I met at [Degnan's] political/socialite dinner parties," Solomon recently recalled. "There were lots of parties in those days." Hinckle's office was bedlam back then, so to be able to work without constant interruptions, "Warren and I worked mostly at my office at 1620 Montgomery Street. Warren arrived with piles of copy and loose photos and we put it all together, page after page, on my desks and floor."

Solomon's *Scanlan's* design was unique for counterculture publications at the time. Although Swiss Modernism was a common corporate design language, it was foreign in this context. Solomon said she practiced "Swiss graphics as I learned from Armin Hofmann in Basel. Warren was familiar with the work I did," which included the SFMOMA monthly bulletins, books for Lawrence Halprin, brochures and covers for New Directions. "He had a sharp eye for design but never told me what to do." And then there was the *Scanlan's* logo, with its distinct apostrophe. "It was intentional," she says. "I always designed big punctuation marks. I think I drew it for some reason and Warren said, 'That's it.'"

Ultimately, *Scanlan's* became best known for featuring articles by Hunter S. Thompson, who invented gonzo journalism (later a mainstay of *Rolling Stone*). It was also known for its banned "Guerrilla Issue," which included a picture of President Nixon having lunch with a group of businessmen, each with an alleged criminal record. The issue was eventually released by a small printing company in Canada.

While *Scanlan's* folded in 1971, *Ramparts* hobbled on until 1975, when the counterculture in San Francisco went into hibernation—ending a raucous, thrilling, and key moment in publishing and design history.

Originally published in *Print* magazine, Spring 2017.

## DISCUSSION POINTS

- Why was it necessary to have an alternative press?
- How did the alternative press differ from the mainstream?
- Was there a qualitative difference in design between alternative and mainstream?
- Is there an alternative press today?

# The Plastic Wars

We shall fight on the seas and oceans,

We shall fight with growing confidence . . .

We shall fight on the beaches,

We shall fight on the landing grounds,

We shall fight in the fields and in the streets,

We shall fight in the hills;

We shall never surrender.

Winston Churchill's famous rallying call urging England to resist the Nazi threat of world domination has resonance today. I don't mean to suggest a false equivalency, but right now we are involved in a new war. Plastic is a world-dominating enemy—and all of us are complicit. Even the most conscientious recyclers succumb to the convenience of plastic and allow its monopoly on our lifestyles to challenge our resolve.

Who doesn't recoil at the gruesome photographs of birds strangled by plastic six-pack rings and dead fish with innards filled with plastic refuse? It is impossible to find waterfronts free of floating plastic containers. Plastic is everywhere. Restrictions have had some impact on consumption, plastic bags are gradually being banned in many states and replaced by reusable totes, and plastic soda bottles fill the recycling bins (and produce income for bottle hoarders). However, plastics are an incontrovertible fact of life *and* death— we seem incapable of shaking the habit or getting along without them.

For those who recall Mike Nichols's 1967 film *The Graduate*, the hero, disillusioned twenty-one-year-old Benjamin Braddock (Dustin Hoffman), is at a cocktail party his parents have thrown to celebrate his graduation from college. A friend of his upper-middle-class mom and dad takes Ben aside to give him one word of wisdom for the future. "Plastics," he says. Yet, rather than better living through the wonders of postwar science, in 1967 "plastics" suggested a cheap, ugly, and vapid way of life—the embodiment of every value of the older generation that is repugnant to Ben (and youth culture in general).

This existential rebellion notwithstanding, plastic took over the world in virtually every mass-produced product and likewise became one of the world's most unbiodegradable disposables. Inventions for producing all sorts of gimmicks are still being made from the stuff, like handy watermelon-carrying cases.

Don't think I'm throwing stones. I'm plastical. At this very moment, I am drinking my morning iced tea from a plastic cup marked with the recycling logo with #1 (PETE—Polyethylene Terephthalate), which is the easiest of plastics to recycle. But sitting around my desk are a few less biodegradable products: #2 (HDPE—High density Polyethylene), #3 (PVC—Polyvinyl Chloride), and #5 (PP—Polypropylene). I probably have #6 and #7 around as well. Like any addict, I swear that if I wanted to I could curtail my use of plastic cups (I'm trying), but plastic straws are more difficult.

"At first glance, bans on plastic straws might seem like a simple—and harmless—next step for the environmentally conscious," wrote the *Guardian* about a proposed California ban. But the battle is far from simple. Advocates for the disabled insist that straws are a necessary aid, and I agree. So why not paper straws, metal, or bamboo? I frequent a few eateries that use paper straws and they work just fine, but not all paper is eco-friendly or biodegradable. In the war against plastic, I've found that not everyone is on the same side—or equally knowledgeable.

I certainly do not have the answers. Recently, I bought an iced tea from a nice little shop in Great Barrington, Massachusetts. The tea came in a plastic cup (the plastic lid was self service). Problem was, there were no straws to be found. When I asked the barista if he had any, his "NO!" felt like a sharp knife in my gut. No explanation, just "NO!" So I walked across the street to another nice shop, where I found a container of straws for the taking. I'm fine with reducing straw consumption for the sake of the environment; But I ain't going to take no attitude from a sanctimonious barista.

Worldwide, entire countries have prohibited plastic straws, with Taiwan working to eliminate all single-use straws by 2025. The United Kingdom and the European Union are considering similar measures.

---

Originally published on *Design Observer*, September 6, 2018.

# DISCUSSION POINTS

- What is a designer's responsibility to the environment?

- How can a designer practice in a responsible and/or sustainable way?

- Should designers have policies regarding the materials they use?

- How can due diligence be practiced in a reasonable or practical way to avoid toxic materials?

# FOUR: BUSINESS AND COMMERCE

# Commercial Art or Whatever You Call It...

Are you a graphics designer? Your business card may say "graphic designer," but in some precincts you are indeed a graphics designer—with emphasis on the "ics." For the longest time that was the designation used in *New York Times* obituaries to describe a deceased commercial artist, layout artist, boardman, communications designer, or graphic designer. For the dead it didn't matter, but for the living . . . It wasn't until after pressure from the design director that the "s" was removed. Nonetheless, it illustrates how the evolution of the word(s) to describe individuals like us who manipulate type and image, communicate visual ideas, or promote products visually has evolved, devolved, and revolved into the entity it is today, which is . . . Well, that's the question. Where has our descriptor evolved to? Let's look at a brief lineage.

When the commercial craft known for type design, typographic makeup, and page layout began in the early nineteenth century, it was ostensibly executed by printers who had their own nomenclature. What to specifically call the layout people on the printing staff was confusing because many were printer's devils (apprentices who did a little of everything). The journeymen or experienced printers "composed" the type and pages, but the evolutionarily advanced layout people were not solely "compositors," which was the designation for a craftsman who more or less followed a layout that was sketched out by an editor or advertising agent or printing representative. These layout people did something more—let's call it design.

Layout people who made roughs, comps, or sketches were soon pulled from the pressroom and placed into the boardroom, where they worked at a drafting board. It was then, around the turn of the century, that the design profession began slowly to emerge from the primal ooze. Layout people were unofficially called boardmen (mostly men but some women too). Nonetheless, the operative term around the 1890s was "commercial artist."

"Art" was the term for any kind of pictorial material used in printing. It wasn't a value judgement, but a fact: "Let's get some art to fill the page." To distinguish high from low art—meaning gallery and museum art from reproduction art—the word "commercial" was invoked to imply less noble status. It was the job of the art editor to commission art. The first reference to an art *director* that I found was Clark Hobart for the *Burr McIntosh Monthly* (1903–1910), which also had an art editor. Hobart's job was to fill the pages with art that he sketched out or designed for the compositor.

The professional terms continued to splinter throughout the early twentieth century. There were book designers, poster artists (*affichistes*), advertising artists, illustrators, and more. Add to that some of the foreign terms: *gebrauchsgrafiker, grafisch ontwerper, grafiste*, etc. But on August 29, 1922, W. A. Dwiggins, in "New Kind of Printing Calls for New Design" in the *Boston Evening Transcript*, used the phrase "graphic designer" to describe his own work as illustrator, advertising artist, calligrapher, typographer, type designer, and book designer. The term was not widely circulated at the time, but would crop up again and again during the 1930s and '40s. "Commercial artist" was still the dominant term—even Paul Rand proudly referred to his own practice with the title. "To see the commercial artist as nothing but a pitchman is a little too glib," he said in *American Artist* (October 1970). "What about the special skills of the commercial artist, his way with type and typography, his knowledge of reproduction processes, his design ability, his showmanship . . . and, yes, his salesmanship."

What we call ourselves is part of that showmanship and salesmanship. Funnily, just as the average person has become aware of graphic design (thanks to the personal computer), the terminology is again in an evolutionary state. The AIGA no longer calls itself the American Institute of Graphic Arts because not only is it too arcane to say "graphic arts," but to say American Institute of Graphic Design would not encompass all the new disciplines (and require a new logo).

The digital revolution has reshaped the landscape, the terminology, and the practice. Today, "commercial artist" is quaint. But "visual communicator," "visual designer," "information architect," or "content designer" seem strained. "Digital designer" and "data visualizer" are more up to date, but unsatisfying. "Graphic designer," while not entirely satisfactory, is nonetheless comfortable. Maybe we should take a cue from the medical profession: all doctors are doctors, but they have their specialties too. So how about "Graphic Designer/ Typologist" or "Graphic Designer/DataVizualist"? Or maybe, in the name of keeping life simple: "Graphic Designer"?

Originally published in *Print* magazine, June 2014.

# DISCUSSION POINTS

- Does it matter what you call your profession?
- What is the most accurate title for what you do?
- How have graphic and other design disciplines altered the way designers practice?
- What are you? And why?

# A Designer by Any Other Name

Since graphic design is not a licensed profession, we can call ourselves anything we want, with the exception of maybe "doctor" or "monsignor" (although Monsignor Dr. Heller has a nice ring). Likewise, anyone can claim the graphic designer mantle (or "graphics designer," which is the dead giveaway that they're not graphic designers), without an iota of schooling, simply because they made a letterhead, newsletter, or website on their home computer. If our nomenclature is this fungible, then it stands to reason our bona fides are in question too, at least in the eyes of the outsider looking in and even the insider looking out. A designer by any other name may still be a designer, yet make no mistake: what we call ourselves is key to our professional health and well-being. As professionals we are hired to be clarifiers, organizers, and even namers for our clients. If we don't know what to call us, who does?

# "Does anyone here call themselves commercial artists?"

Nonetheless, given the current growing intersection of graphic design with time-based media, information design, and other associated disciplines, including writing and producing, as well as blurring boundaries between fine art and design, who and what we are (and ultimately want to be) is becoming more complicated to define, and therefore to name. Yet it wasn't always this confounding.

Before W. A. Dwiggins famously coined the term *graphic design* in a 1922 Boston newspaper article as a means to describe the wide range of jobs he personally tackled, "commercial artist" was the accepted label for the interrelated acts of drawing, speccing, comping, and laying out. Dwiggins, however, was a jack of many graphic trades, including but not limited to illustrating books, composing pages, designing typefaces (including Metro and Caledonia), and producing calligraphic hand lettering, stencil ornament, book covers and jackets, book interiors and title pages, advertising and journal formats, along with handbills, stationery, labels, and signs, not to mention writing his own critical essays, fiction stories, and marionette plays. Being an iconoclast, he wanted to distinguish his activities from more humdrum, less prolific commercial artists and coined a term that was uniquely his own. Graphic design, which was derived from—but was much broader than— "graphic arts" (signifying drawing and engraving) defined such a personally esoteric pursuit that Dwig could not have predicted that decades later graphic design would become the standard professional description. Although he never actually called himself a "graphic designer," his coinage was cast like bread upon the sea and eventually washed up on professional shores.

I recently asked for a show of hands at an AIGA/New York student conference (which I moderated) on the nexus of commerce and passion in answer to the question "Does anyone here call themselves commercial artists?" Predictably, not one among these college juniors and seniors raised their hands. But surprisingly, only two-thirds of them embraced the term "graphic designer," and a few of them were rather tentative. Over a decade ago, when schools and design firms started affixing loftier monikers to academic degrees and business cards, the most common newbie was "communications design," which along with "graphic communications" and "visual communications" (or the martial-sounding Viz-Com) seemed to address the transition from old to new media. A little while later, thanks to Richard Saul Wurman in a milestone talk before the first AIGA Conference in Boston, the field was given his quixotic appellation, "information architects." In the mid- to late 1990s, when the web became a dominant presence in design practice, this tag became much more commonly applied, along with "user interface designers," "human centered interface designers," and "experiential interface designers." All of a sudden, the name game turned into something of an Olympics to outdo the next guy, with designers adding all sorts of in-your-face or interface verbiage to their credentials.

Currently there is something of a schism between a newly coined and curiously pejorative term, "conventional designer," which indicates a solely print orientation, and other art/techno/science-sounding job descriptions. The first time I ever heard the term "conventional design" it was uttered by a guru in the "web standards" movement, who was obviously trying to drive a wedge by making a huge distinction between web designers and print designers—who, by implication, were designosaurs (try that on your business card—or website).

If graphic design is synonymous with print, and print is "conventional," then a priori anything in the nonprint realm is "unconventional." While this makes linguistic sense, the last time I looked, print was still a vital medium in which many progressive designers continue to experiment with type and image in brilliant ways. In theory, the web and other digital platforms are the proverbial new frontier, but in practice too much "standardized" web design (i.e., the major news and commercial sites from Amazon to the

BBC) is replete with—and at times drowning in—brand-spanking-new conventions. Achieving comparably great design on the web has yet to happen. What's more, whether on the page or screen, designers are still making graphic things. Still, the term "graphic design" is on its way to becoming obsolete. (Full disclosure: even the School of Visual Arts New York City's MFA Designer as Author program, which I cochair, dropped the "graphic" when it began almost ten years ago to indicate more than just print studies.) Some "conventional" designers even buy into the designosaur concept. Recently, I heard a highly reputed print designer announce that the end of printed books is near, to be replaced by the "tablet" or digital reader, a technological advancement that will allow pages to be read like print but in pixel form, and end the need for book or book cover/jacket designers, perhaps in favor of a new job description, "tablet-interface designers." With the evolutionary onslaught of new tech already upon us, the day may come when designers will be called "ologists," as in designologists, typologists, or "interfaceologists."

It's not so farfetched to think that in a few years' time the academies and profession will totally sweep out all the old nomenclature—as it did "commercial art"—for labels that completely alter and elevate the outside and inside perceptions of what we do and who we are. For instance, a number of the students attending the AIGA conference told me they "do branding," which incorporates graphic, web, and experiential design in one total, integrated package. So I asked them, what do they call this field in their classes? The answer was Brand Specialists—not too far from my anticipated answer, brandologists—which eliminated the words "graphic" and "design" entirely.

Back in 1993, citing a "dysfunctional name" out of touch with the times and technologies, the AIGA—originally founded in 1913 as the American Institute of Graphic Arts—considered calling itself the American Institute of Graphic Design. Massimo Vignelli said about the venerable moniker, "So the name AIGA has been around for eighty years. Even if it had been around for a thousand years, it would still be wrong." Yet despite a wellspring of lobbying to change, the naming committees soon rejected the inclusion of the word "graphic," fearing it would be out of date by the time the letterhead was redesigned. AIGA is no longer initials but a melody, with the qualifying

*It's not so farfetched to think that in a few years' time the academies and profession will totally sweep out all the old nomenclature— as it did "commercial art..."*

subtitle "The Professional Organization for Design" suggesting there are many sub-professions under (or perhaps replacing) the broad rubric of what was once graphic design. Which makes sense in this radically integrated new media world—although, truth be known, I still like the word "graphic," if only for the comfort it provides.

Funnily, not all the students attending the AIGA/New York conference knew exactly what the initials AIGA stood for, nor did they much care. Knowing it is the "Professional Organization for Design" was enough for their immediate needs. But like the organization itself, which is in the process of looking toward the future, these students face a naming (or rather branding) conundrum. How, through their names and labels, do they telegraph what they do? With such a growing menu of terms to choose from, maybe "graphic designer" is, at least, not so nebulous, while clearly for many it's incredibly confining.

Which leads to another profound shift: These very new media causing an identity crisis are also enabling designers to do more independent, authorial, or entrepreneurial work. For previous generations, independence was daunting. But now, all that prevents a designer from inventing, fabricating, and selling unique wares is a lack of talent, ingenuity, and drive. I know some undergrads, and many of my own graduate students, who have made products for the marketplace. So what do we call ourselves when the practice shifts from service provider to producer? Maybe my own story will have some resonance.

When I first started out, forty years ago, I called myself a cartoonist. When that went sour because my talents were limited, I became a graphic designer, but really I was an art director, which is how I labeled myself for over thirty-five years. An art director, by the way, is one of those jobs that even a non–graphic (or graphics) designer can do, as long as she knows how to collaborate with designers, photographers, and illustrators. In 2007, I quit being an art director. The worst part of the decision was not leaving a job I loved to broaden my horizons, but coming up with a new title to identify myself. Since I've been writing articles and books, I thought I might call myself "graphic writer," but that sounds almost as archaic as "commercial artist." So I thought "ex–art director" sounded appropriate, until I realized it was like "ex-husband" and was too negative. "Para-designer" has a nice cadence, but lacks meaning. Since I work with students, "design educator" had the right ring, but is also too limiting for what I do. "Design impresario" is too pretentious, and "design consultant" sounds like a non-job. "Interface engineer" doesn't quite sync with my purpose in life. And I think "design slut" is taken. So as of this writing I no longer have a title, and though I still think of myself as a graphic designer, I worry that without a tag that defines me in relation to my peers and betters, I will simply be a former professional. A designer by any other name is still a designer, but it's important to have a viable name, whatever it may be.

Originally published as "What Do We Call Ourselves Now?" in *EYE* magazine, issue no. 63, Spring 2007.

## DISCUSSION POINTS

- What do you identify as professionally? What do you call yourself?
- Does a job category have significance?
- How have the changes in technology and overall responsibility changed the definition of the profession?
- What is the most important factor in being a graphic designer?

# What a Way to Earn a Living

"Commercial art is a business. It is bought mostly for business purposes, and its cost is entered as a business expense on any company's books. Because artwork is a competitive product that serves a business function, it should be promoted and sold in the most businesslike manner possible. But it is also something much more." So wrote Fred Charles Rodewald in his 1954 book *Commercial Art as a Business*.

It is more than likely that most readers of this essay have never heard of Rodewald (1905–1955). Yet he served as an important role model in his day. Rodewald was primarily an illustrator, which included the art of lettering. He took it seriously. In fact, he advocated for commercial artists' rights to be professional—a pioneer in fair labor practices, you might say—and was a leader of the Artists Guild of New York. *Commercial Art as a Business* is a guide to the practical concerns of earning a living as a commercial artist.

He covered pricing, financing, bookkeeping, law, and sales. In his introduction, Rodewald cited the census data showing that there were approximately 80,000 artists in the United States, nearly 20,000 in and near New York, 7,000 in Chicago, and 6,000 in Los Angeles, with the total in other cities rarely exceeding 2,500. However, in his day, there were no well-paying salaried art jobs—yet with thousands of newspapers and magazines, illustrated ads, posters, billboards, booklets, folders, and the like, there was freelance gold in them there hills. "Our bookstores, libraries, classrooms, and homes contain millions of books and pamphlets filled with pictorial matter of every description," he wrote. "The clothes we wear, the houses we live in, the countless gadgets we use—all bear the marks of artistic effort."

"Commercial art, regardless of its ultimate use," he continued, "remains basically an art—not in any precious or esoteric sense, but because fundamentally it meets with the specifications that apply to all art." No, commercial art may not pack an artistic wallop like the Sistine Chapel murals, but they do have something in common: both were done on commission for a client (and the client was God).

Back in Rodewald's time, commercial artists who received salaries of $10,000 were usually in some executive capacity—art directors, art managers, art buyers—not producers of art. The salaried job was just a stepping-stone to better things. How many successful commercial artists started as job-holders? Well, I couldn't tell you. But many sat behind desks, making Solomonic decisions between one illustrator and another, until they realized they could do it just as good or better, and get the dough.

Rodewald spent most of his career *doing* rather than managing commercial art, so he decided that it was important to share his knowledge with up-and-comers. He wrote eloquently about existential things like time, ethics, and even why artwork should be signed. He also shared insight on shortcuts, selling, pricing, and what to expect from art directors. But the most revealing chapter is "Kickbacks and Favoritism," a fact of professional life back then that is little discussed in 2018 (is it?).

It is easy to think that whatever our field is called today, it has not changed much since Rodewald published his book in 1954. But the excerpt below is unusual (isn't it?).

There are doubtless art directors and other buyers who extort rebates in return for giving out work. Such kickbacks may range all the way from a fixed percentage of every billing to occasional gratuities in the form of cash, or Christmas and birthday presents of great enough value to place them outside the category of harmless amenities.

Such practices are nothing short of bribery and racketeering, and are not only harmful and costly to the artists, but also to the employers of the guilty individuals. . . . In most states they also constitute a crime.

Section 439 of the New York Penal Code defines as a misdemeanor and describes with fair accuracy the type of kickback familiar in the art business, and provides penalties of up to $500 and one year in jail for both parties to the deal . . .

Because evil casts its ugly shadow indiscriminately over all, it should be the concern of all. . . . It is therefore a matter of elementary prudence for all art buyers to maintain a reasonable appearance of impartiality as well as to practice it. An art director who plays favorites, and who sometimes goes as far to indicate that he will buy the work of an artist only if handled through a certain studio or representative, must not be surprised if it is rumored that he is receiving kickbacks, regardless of how unfounded such accusations may be . . .

Aside from painstaking correctness in all his dealings involving artists, a good art buyer sees to it, if only in the strictest self-interest, that the artwork he buys is handled fairly and honestly all down the line.

———————————————

Originally published as "Commercial Art: What a Way to Earn a Living" on *Design Observer*, December 5, 2018.

# DISCUSSION POINTS

- What is the value of professional ethics?

- What are the "best practices" of today's design field?

- Is it necessary for designers to develop standards if they are starting a business?

- Do professional ethics play a role in contemporary practice?

*Typefaces are integral to how we all communicate, yet the average digital type consumers accept default fonts without having question or clue about the fine points of type or typography, and they cannot discern original from pirated or plagiarized fonts. Rampant type illiteracy and complacency contributes to the rash of typographic identity theft, underscored by digital piracy—using a typeface that the user hasn't paid for—and plagiarism—the act of passing off someone else's work as one's own. Some violators think just because they make minor adjustments, they are getting away with something. Wrong!*

# Identity Theft Can Destroy Type Families

Creating original type and type families has become a big business, so emotions run high among type designers over the impact that piracy and plagiarism have on the field, the culture, and their livelihoods. Indeed, most type designers have experienced theft of their work at one time or another. While some of them vigilantly combat offenders, others are resigned to a practice that dates back to when printing master Aldus Manutius's 1501 italic was copied by Balthazar de Gabiano from Lyon, who popularized it in

France. "I think if some design is perceived as successful," says New York–based type designer James Montalbano, "someone will attempt to knock it off."

Other common reasons for piracy and plagiarism include greed or the need to reduce costs. "For the most part," says Frank Martinez, a Brooklyn-based intellectual property lawyer who specializes in typeface cases, "type font infringement occurs due to commercial considerations or expedience on the part of the infringer." Students are notorious for finding illegal ways to use fonts or resort to free fonts, many of which are lame copies of the real thing.

Protections against innocent and devious type infringement are not foolproof and take effort to police. "The initial responsibility to preserve a property right lies squarely with the owner," explains Martinez, who adds that while England officially recognized the right to copyright for typefaces in 1916, "In the US the design of the typeface cannot be protected, but the software creating the designs is considered copyrightable subject matter." If that is evident, action can be taken.

Typeface theft soared when digitization geared up in the late 1980s. The digital foundry P22 made a concerted effort to contact websites and group hosts "as soon as we became aware that a simple DCMA (Digital Millennium Copyright Act) takedown notification is the weapon of choice and they have to comply," explains P22's Carima El-Behairy, "otherwise they themselves become liable of hosting—trading illegal software [dating] as early as 1997."

Most piracy comes from font-sharing sites, which El-Behairy targeted and says should suffer stiffer penalties when caught with pirated software. "Canada has a zero tolerance for piracy and the government actually conducts the audits," she says. But regarding penalties, Peter Bilak of the Dutch-based Fontstand feels that laws cannot change anything, and it is up to designers to rethink font licensing. "The only way to fight the piracy is to make alternative products more accessible and affordable," he explains. "This is what Fontstand is doing, making high-quality fonts easy to license, rather than covered by extra protection schemes."

Meanwhile, Rudy VanderLans, co-founder of Emigre Fonts and a veteran of piracy wars, admonishes students and businesses alike: "Don't steal from others. I know it's not that simple, but if you absolutely have to 'appropriate' the work of others, and you're in doubt whether it's legal, ask for permission. You'd be surprised how easy that is, and how it can be mutually beneficial." Both VanderLans and Bilak state that rather than endure the costly consequences of piracy, they are willing to find common ground with violators who could become their future customers.

Open-source advocates may have differing views about the sanctity of original typeface ownership, particularly since many typeface designs are frequently based on—or are revisions of—antique models. But designers have long held that typefaces are works in progress and improvements are inevitable.

"Creating a new face based upon an old design is usually referred to as a 'revival,'" says Martinez. "Generally speaking, the primary rationale is to create a digital version of an otherwise unavailable (out of publication) typeface. A second motivating factor may be a desire to modernize a typeface, adding new 'glyphs' and sometimes a foreign language version." How much can or should be changed? Martinez says that in the United States, there is no minimum requirement. "However, if a competing digital revival exists, the software cannot be used since such use comprises copyright infringement."

Type designers commonly believe that the basic rationale for making a new version is when a type design does not yet exist in a digital format or if they can build a better classic face for the current technology. El-Behairy asserts that the only exceptions are when variations on a typeface are appropriate. "Only if it corrects a design flaw or to allow it to work in a specific application or fix a size constraint." Another rule of thumb is that the source material be older than seventy years plus the life of the artist. El-Behairy adds, "We try to remain as true to the original design as possible; if this is not possible, missing letters, too many variations, we break down the project to allow as many of these variations to be available in a single cohesive typeface, sometimes creating new letters to match." Montalbano explains that he uses historical reference as a starting point and tries to move on from there but that there will invariably be similarities to basic models: "Type design is a fashion business in a way. Every designer should have their version of the little black dress, the three-piece suit, formal wear, casuals, etc. Type design is no different—there are basic historical genres that underpin all type design."

Monotype's New York director, Dan Rhatigan, concurs that the rationale for a new digital version of an old analog type is a matter of realizing that the old design is not necessarily suitable for current needs. "For instance, when Monotype considers revivals of old metal-type designs or updates to what is already available as digital type, it's usually about seeing that there's commercial potential to a design that people are interested in." Older designs generally have inherent problems that come from the constraints of how they were first produced, which demands revival. But, Rhatigan adds, "Even digital type can usually be improved or expanded upon. In short, if we base a new product on an older design, it's because that design wasn't enough, in some way."

Jonathan Hoefler, founder of the New York foundry H&Co, has spent considerable effort policing violators of his proprietary fonts, many of which were based on vintage models. He likens the designing of a historical typographic revival to directing a motion picture that's based on a work of literature. "When we at H&Co create a typeface that's inspired by historical forms—whether it's a sixteenth-century printing type like the one that inspired Quarto, or a style of sign making as was the case for Gotham— we never, ever begin with an existing font."

This means that the design team explores the ideas behind a collection of "physical artifacts" from the past and reinterprets them as "a family of digital fonts," which pulls the process away from mere copying and allows room for originality on many levels. Hoefler adds that "fonts are made of drawings (not scans or tracings), character sets demand more glyphs than any historical artifact ever offers, and the ways in which type is used today demand not just attractive alphabets, but coherent systems of related styles (whether they're weights or widths or romans and italics), all of which are up to the modern designer to supply."

Why is theft more common than in analog days? When it comes to piracy, Montalbano says that there might be the "hobby/collector" mentality at work. But more likely, "I do think that there is an 'everything on the internet should be free' attitude. Certainly companies like Google who offer "libre" fonts are not helping things."

"I think it is laziness," says El-Behairy. "Why should they license the original if it is available for free, and there is a prevailing attitude that fonts do not have the value as other software so why should they pay for it?"

"I think greed plays a smaller part than ever before," adds Rhatigan. "It's usually a case of ignorance about licensing and copyright, or laziness about how to go about exploring a twist on an existing design. Overzealous thrift is probably more to blame now that it is so easy to copy digital data, and so temptingly easy to just open up a file and begin tinkering with it to make it something else."

It's hard to say whether plagiarism is on the rise or not, says Hoefler. Instead, he lists four typeface design warnings against stealing: "It's not financially rewarding, it's not artistically satisfying, it's legally perilous, and that in a creative industry like ours, it's a career killer." While the average consumer may be blind, the seasoned professional can spot a knockoff, and nobody respects a plagiarist. "You don't become a good designer by modifying someone else's fonts. . . . And you miss out on all the creative satisfaction that comes from having a point of view, identifying challenges, and satisfying them."

But piracy and plagiarism, like the personal form of identity theft, have their own momentum. So when digital typefaces are the object of theft, Martinez advises that a copyright action is the best recourse. Sometimes notification by way of a cease-and-desist and discussions can remove the need to file a lawsuit. Yet care should be taken to ensure that actual copying of software exists. "Remember," he says, "since the designs cannot be copyrighted, anyone is free to just re-create the designs, provided they don't copy the software."

Previously unpublished.

## DISCUSSION POINTS

- Do you view typefaces and fonts as intellectual property?
- How should typefaces and fonts be protected from unauthorized use?
- What is the difference between open-source and licensed type fonts?
- How do you feel about open-source property?

# Flipping
# My Lid

Like Pavlov's compliant canine, I salivate whenever I see someone walking down the street holding a paper coffee cup topped with a Solo Travel lid. The various other varieties of flat plastic covers, including some that look like the starship *Enterprise*, don't move me at all (and Styrofoam cups are a total turnoff), but the paper ones crowned with small upturned protruding spouts make me want to bark at the moon—I mean, savor a hot beverage. I don't actually drink coffee, but a viable substitute that suits my craving for the cup and topper is a calorie-laden chai soy latte. I can taste the alluringly sweet herbal flavor simply by looking at the lid. (Incidentally, the same drink in a ceramic mug or china cup does not produce even an iota of that Pavlovian sensation.)

Why does this particular plastic lid, designed by Jack Clements, trigger such a strong cognitive and emotive response? Why do I flip my lid whenever I see one? Although I hate to think that I am just a lab rat (or dog) that proves a marketing theory, which ultimately determines how designers design for mass consumption—oh how I hate the pseudoscience of market research— the truth is, I am exactly that person. I'm the kind of hardwired character who succumbs to the behavioral manipulation of everyday designed things— many of which have been forged in the bowels of testers' laboratories. For instance, I don't buy food packages with the color blue, rarely relate to brands with "V" in the name, and avoid cake mix that doesn't show a delicious wedge cut from its heart—what's more, I'm a sucker for fake droplets on cans of Coors (and I don't even drink beer). The Solo lids surge right through whatever defenses I might still have.

Although it is officially called a "sanitary lid," which implies a loftier social purpose, I don't care about such highfalutin things when something more primal is at play. The Solo lid returns me to those days when subliminal advertising was the norm (I still can recall the fresh coffee aroma emanating from the Chock Full O' Nuts sign in Times Square). I can't help being drawn to it for corporeal reasons. Every time I vow not to be held hostage to compulsion, forces beyond my control take charge.

Here come the inevitable Freudian references: The Solo Travel lid is a substitute for a mother's breast—what we might call nature's original travel lid. The flat covers with the tear-back openings offer no such metaphoric representation. Instead, spout = nipple. Paper cup = warm skin. Coffee, tea, or soy = mother's milk. Ergo, the lid is a nurturing apparatus. It provides comfort and joy as well as nourishment. Certainly plastic is not the most warm and loving material, but somehow the fundamental shape transcends the emotive limitations of the materials. Somehow that spout or lozenge-shaped opening is a means to a totally satisfying end.

I've tried to analyze my fixation through other filters. Does it matter who is holding the cup? Not at all—my interest is not user-specific. Does it matter what color the cup is? No, although I prefer white or brown. Does it matter what color the lid is? I've only suckled from white and black lids, but I would not like blue or red. Does it matter what's in the cup? Obviously not!

For most people a cover, to paraphrase Freud, is just a cover—simply functional. The Solo Travel lid is easier to use since there is no fumbling around with the tab. Yet, on the downside, it is not self-sealing. I've noticed that sophisticated baristas wastefully use two of them, slightly turned in opposite directions, in order to close the opening. For me this cover is not just an old everyday thing. It is a special everyday thing that brings happiness to my heart and steamed soy to my lips.

Originally published as "Graphic Content | Flipping My Lid" in *T: The New York Times Style Magazine*, March 3, 2010.

## DISCUSSION POINTS

- Is designing a coffee lid a useful use of one's talents?
- Can the "perfect" lid somehow save the planet?
- When takeout cups began, the lid was paper. Was that better for the environment?
- Do graphic and product designers have a responsibility for environmentally safe design?

*Decades before digital media spawned the "information age," there were colossal heaps of analog information just begging to be organized into manageable, accessible, and retrievable bundles. Data filled every kind of storage receptacle and facility. Drowning in data during the post–World War II era, American industry called on engineers to create effective systems for its organization. This could not be accomplished without designers, especially graphic designers. The mission to modernize led directly to innovating more efficient communications, expressed through typographic simplicity and compositional ingenuity. One of the leaders of this design "crusade" was the Czech-born Ladislav Sutnar (1897–1976), a graphic, product, furniture, and exhibition designer and educator.*

# Catalog Design Progress Is Still Progressive

In 1939, while on a trip to the United States, having been commissioned to design the interior exhibition space for the Czech pavilion at the New York World's Fair, Nazi Germany invaded Czechoslovakia. Sutnar remained in New York City and would never again return home (until his ashes were brought back to Plzeň decades after his death). Before coming to New York, however, Sutnar was a devoted modernist. His output of printed and typographic work was both disciplined and hierarchical, exemplifying the asymmetrical ethos of the progressive New Typography. His work invoked simplicity while addressing complexity of the industrial world. By the time he came to New York, he was well suited to pioneer a new genre of graphic information design that would prove beneficial to industry, especially for builders, engineers, and architects.

It may seem minor, but Sutnar's achievement was the transformation of the common trade or industrial catalog from a chaotic array of material to a wieldy (and sublimely beautiful) system that saved time and energy. It was a major breakthrough for industry that might not have happened had Sutnar not met and collaborated with another visionary, Danish-born Knud Lönberg-Holm.

Lönberg-Holm's name is little known today. He was an architect, photographer, designer, writer, and teacher in his own right. Engaged in avant-garde European design circles, he worked with Gropius, Buckminster Fuller, El Lissitzky, and others in the modern movement. In 1924 he was invited by the University of Michigan to teach an elementary architecture and design course, where he was an enthusiastic propagandist for modernism. Between 1927 and 1929, he served on the editorial board of *The Architectural Record*, the voice of the modern sensibility then on the rise in America. He was responsible for the magazine's "Technical News and Research Section," which drew not just from the usual architectural literature, but also, uniquely, from the tradition of scientific discourse. From science he borrowed the idea of using graphic charts and diagrams to effectively clarify complex issues regarding such subjects as building types and environmental control technology. He became a member of the Congress for International Modern Architecture (CIMA), whose membership notably included Walter Gropius, Serge Chermayeff, Marcel Breuer, and

*Their philosophy on designing information—today called data visualization or information architecture—was rooted in clean, clear, and concise visual and verbal language.*

Le Corbusier. Over the years, his modernist-urbanist philosophy grew to embrace all design activity, particularly information management, as potential forces for the betterment of human life. It was at a CIMA meeting in the late 1930s where he was introduced to Sutnar.

Lönberg-Holm was employed as publicity director of Sweet's Catalog Service, a publisher that served as a kind of middleman between suppliers and manufacturers to builders and designers. The service, founded in 1906, made hardware and product catalogs of all kinds available, first in one massive volume and then through series of annually updated binders that were fixtures in most contractors' and architects' offices.

Hired by Chauncey L. Williams, vice president of Sweet's parent company, F. W. Dodge Corporation, to unify the disparate catalogs that they distributed, Lönberg-Holm defined the problem as a need for clarity and accessibility and proposed to solve it through navigational design aids and reductive language, akin to today's approach to wireless web and mobile design. Toward this aim, Lönberg-Holm wrote countless memoranda detailing a sophisticated process of design standardization. In order to make this concrete, he needed a graphic designer with similar convictions. Sutnar's reputation in Europe preceded him to New York. So, after the two met, Lönberg-Holm convinced Williams to hire Sutnar as design director for research.

Lönberg-Holm was the other half of Sutnar's brain. Their philosophy on designing information—today called data visualization or information architecture—was rooted in clean, clear, and concise visual and verbal language. What Gilbert and Sullivan were to light opera or Rogers and Hammerstein were to the Broadway musical, Lönberg-Holm and Sutnar were to data orchestration. Together they composed *Catalog Design* (1944) and *Catalog Design Progress* (1950). The former introduced a variety of systematic departures in catalog design; the latter fine-tuned those models to show how complex information could be organized and, most importantly, retrieved.

Almost seventy years after its publication, *Catalog Design Progress* is an archetype for functional design—and in many ways fundamentally holds up today.

Throughout their working relationship, Sutnar continued running in his own design firms, with other partners for other clients (including Bell Telephone Co., for whom he designed the prototype of the area code). Yet for four hours each day, from about 11:00 a.m. to 2:00 p.m., he worked in Sweet's offices on West Fortieth Street (entering and exiting through a service elevator, for some curious reason). The pair met daily to hash out ways to simplify their customers' access to thousands of supplies, from screws to roofing to plumbing fixtures, in the Sweet's compilations. First among many tasks was to painstakingly rewrite the dreadful catalog copy. They also agreed that every user comprehends information differently, so they devised mechanisms, what Sutnar called "active design elements," to offer multiple entry or access points for each kind of user.

An index was conceived to cross-reference each object in three ways: by company name, by trade or brand name, and by the name of the objects (i.e. "windows"). Lonberg-Holm further observed that while objects routinely change (i.e. "windows," "sliders," "portholes"), activities remain constant (i.e. "glazing"), and urged that this classification also be included as an organizing element. Sutnar and Lönberg-Holm shared the same logic: Both were philosophical constructivists with practical leanings. Their habitual search for perfect form led them to deconstruct every potential form so as to reframe and synthesize the ideas underneath the forms. It was an article of faith that there could be no confusion in the presentation. So in determining the best format, they moved from word (Lönberg-Holm) to design and image (Sutnar), merging the ideas into a seamless whole. At times they intensely debated the meaning of a single word or the placement of a single picture. Each so revered precision that though arguments inevitably flared (once Sutnar stopped speaking to Lönberg-Holm for a month over a point of language), they ultimately agreed.

Sutnar's first task was to redefine Sweet's corporate identity. He refreshed the company's logo, changing from a Victorian-style nameplate (typical of many older American businesses and institutions) to a sans-serif S within a bold circle (indicative of the modern style). Sutnar also designed the binders and introduced tabbed divider pages. While these departures demonstrated a change in attitude and approach, the most concrete and definitive explanation of their mission was given in three books, which today are holy grails of information design.

Together they conceived and wrote *Catalog Design* in 1944 to introduce various systematic departures in contemporary catalog design. *Designing Information*, published in 1947, was a test version of their 1950 book, the even more ambitious *Catalog Design Progress*, which was dedicated to making product selection simpler and the flow of information through various media faster. Each was designed as a manual/guidebook to initiate the uninitiated into the belief that "good" graphic design is a panacea for jumbled thinking. *Catalog Design* was a guide-cum-manifesto written to encourage the catalog designers who contributed to Sweet's collection to follow more rigorous standards of organization, while allowing them to have distinctive designs. From today's vantage point, the ideas seem fairly simple, but at a time when most trade and industrial catalogs were a potpourri of miscellaneous pictures fitted with as little space as possible between lengthy descriptions and item numbers, the notion that text and image could be framed by white space, or that a catalog could benefit from grid layouts, was tantamount to revolution. In a 1947 memorandum to Sweet's management concerning their next project, *Designing Information*, Lönberg-Holm

*Underlying Sutnar's modern mission was the desire to introduce aesthetics into, say, a plumber's life.*

anticipated the designer's role in the information age when he wrote: "the simplification of any information, implies simplification of the visual task through clarity and precision-a functional goal of information design." Although Sutnar and Lönberg-Holm did not coin the term "information design," *Designing Information* codified the tenets of clarity and accessibility like no book before it. "The treatment of the subject came about through our realization of the need to clarify design in everyday terms, and to demonstrate that design has practical values that go far beyond mere decoration," Lönberg-Holm wrote.

Sutnar was one of the first editorial designers to design double spreads rather than single pages, an aspect of his methodology that is so common today that in retrospect, the fact that it was an innovation could easily be overlooked. Perhaps Sutnar's most significant innovation in the design of the book itself was his use of full-spread designs. A casual perusal of Sutnar's designs for everything from catalogs to brochures from 1941 on, with the exception of covers, reveals a preponderance of spreads on which his signature navigational devices force the users to follow logically contiguous levels of information. Through these spreads, Sutnar was able to harness certain avant-garde principles and inject visual excitement into even the most routine material without impinging upon accessibility. While his basic structure was decidedly rational, his layout choices—juxtaposition, scale, and color—were rooted in abstraction. They were artful and functional. Underlying Sutnar's modern mission was the desire to introduce aesthetics into, say, a plumber's life.

In the duo's hands, the basic elements of design size, blank space, color, line, etc. were tools for selectivity, simplifying the visual task of the user. *Designing Information* (which was planned as a huge volume, but published in an abridged form) set out to define design as a tool for achieving the "faster flow of information" through principles of flow and unity. Sutnar and Lönberg-Holm took pains to demonstrate the process of visualizing information by including scores of charts and graphs that addressed the needs of customers, employees, stockholders, and the general public. They believed that giving efficient form to information requires more than just pictorial illustration ("Ease of seeing means more than easy to look at," wrote Lönberg-Holm). Their charts became the foundation on which comprehension could be built. In fact, in one simple chart, the whole of *Designing Information* is efficiently summarized as "Transmitting: speed, accessibility; Seeing: visual selectivity, visual continuity; Comprehending: visual extension, universality." This synthesis was the basis of their last collaborative book, *Catalog Design Progress*, a spiral-bound book with a horizontal format that became the design standard for industrial design manuals (and arguably a model for later corporate graphic standards manuals). In it, Holm and Sutnar developed and refined the ideas they had presented in their previous books, showing how complex information could first be organized—and then, more importantly, retrieved.

They addressed specific ways in which levels of information could be organized for easy scanning and gave designers suggestions for maximizing visual interest through symbols, typographic nuances, changes in scale, and so on. Using all the space at his disposal, Sutnar was able to inject excitement into even the most routine material without impinging upon comprehension: his signature navigational devices guided users firmly from one level of information to the next. At the same time, Sutnar was not an invisible designer; he had a style. While his basic structures were decidedly rational, the choices he made in juxtaposition, scale, and color were rooted in sophisticated principles of abstract design, bringing sensitive composition, visual charm, and emotional drama to his workaday subjects. He developed a distinctive vocabulary, or style, notable for arrows, fever lines, black bullets, and other repeated devices. He used all of the above to direct the reader

## *. . . a strong, though not overpowering, design personality can be useful in information design.*

through hierarchies of information, and indeed promoted these devices in *Catalog Design Progress* as the correct forms for guiding readers (which contributed to a kind of Sutnar-biased conformity among later designers).

The fact that Sutnar injected his aesthetic preferences doesn't diminish the effectiveness of his and his partner's ideas. It only goes to show that a strong, though not overpowering, design personality can be useful in information design. Although their landmark work was published in 1950, the pair continued to develop and expand their ideas for another ten years. Sutnar designed many of the trade catalogs that appeared in the Sweet's binder, both as Sweet's staff designer and as a freelance consultant to Sweet's contributors. Chauncey Williams retired in 1960. With his departure, Sweet's golden age, like many design-strong companies before and after, abruptly ended. Sutnar concentrated on his private practice; in consideration of his service, Lonberg-Holm was kept on staff for a year or two more. Once the important work ended, the memory of this collaboration faded. Truly functional graphic design is often ignored—as a result of its defining transparency—while stylish decorative mannerisms are honored in the popular taste.

Although Sutnar and Lönberg-Holm introduced the theoretical constructs that define functional design for information management, the topic was barely addressed by American commercial artists until mid-century corporate modernism took over from earlier avant-garde modernism. Sutnar's contribution to the enlightenment of information design is remembered by the world of design because he left a rich visual legacy, which prefigures current digital media experience designs. His collaborator, if mentioned at all, is brushed off as a philosopher responsible for the invisible structure of their work, rather than a vital contributor to its actual construction. In design histories, Löndberg-Holm's name, though it appears prominently on their books, is somewhat of an appendage to the name Sutnar. He is mentioned as the silent partner. It would be not only more accurate, but more honest, to acknowledge them together. This book is their holy grail and our design treasure.

---

Previously unpublished.

## DISCUSSION POINTS

- What is modernism?
- Why is *Catalog Design Progress* considered modern?
- How well are trade catalogs designed today?
- What was Ladislav Sutnar's lasting contribution to design and commerce?

# Cough, Hack, Cough, Cough

In the smoke-and-mirrors world of advertising of the early twentieth century, cigarette ads seduced women into becoming habitual smokers. No expense was spared to push the myth that sophistication was just a puff away. A series of Lucky Strike magazine ads featured stylized paintings of women decked out in their evening finery. While the graphic design and typography was insignificant, the marriage of persuasive text and evocative image presented in full-color layouts and published in targeted women's magazines was irresistible.

*. . . cigarette advertising promised an altogether better, stress-free, well-proportioned life.*

In "OK Miss America! We thank you for your patronage," a woman wearing a low-cut satin gown is so above the fray that she isn't even holding a Lucky, but the implication is that she had just finished a satisfying smoke. In the haughty "I do" advertisement, a sultry bride pauses for a relaxed smoke and gives her vow to the cigarette of choice.

Cigarettes were marketed as fashion accessories, but these ads, which ran during the Great Depression, were not aimed exclusively at women of means—cigarette advertising promised an altogether better, stress-free, well-proportioned life.

One sales pitch used Henry Wadsworth Longfellow's "First a Shadow Then a Sorrow" to announce Lucky Strike's diet plan. "Avoid that future shadow," the copy suggested, "by refraining from over indulgence. If you would maintain the modern figure of fashion." Under an idealized color painting of a young woman haunted by the shadow of a double chin, the copy read: "We do not represent that smoking Lucky Strike Cigarettes will bring modern figures or cause the reduction of flesh. We do declare that when tempted to do yourself too well, if you will 'Reach for a Lucky' instead, you will thus avoid over indulgence in things that cause excess weight and, by avoiding over indulgence, maintain a modern, graceful form."

Cigarettes were a staple in America. Yet even tobacco manufacturers acknowledged frequent coughing, throat irritation, and raspy voices. The last was, however, promoted as a virtue along with other benefits: "Smokers everywhere are turning to Camels for their delightful 'energizing effect' . . . Camels never get on your nerves." Lucky Strike took the homeopathic route with their motto: "It's toasted." A typical ad read, "Everyone knows that sunshine mellows—that's why the 'toasting' process includes the use of Ultra Violet Rays . . . Everyone knows that heat purifies and so 'toasting'—that extra secret process—removes harmful irritants that cause throat irritation and coughing."

Movie stars and starlets frequently appeared as spokespersons in ads. In a 1943 advertisement, Betty Grable, star of the movie *Pin Up Girl*, is shown in a soldiers' barracks, reinforcing the idea that Chesterfield is overseas "With the boys." To soldiers, cigarettes were as valuable as rations; to the tobacco industry, the war was a boon. Ads invoked the image of American boys, exploited the image of American girls, and portrayed cigarettes as American as apple pie.

The cigarette ads created during the Great Depression and World War II were not beautifully designed or smartly composed, but they effectively targeted women with one purpose: to seduce by appealing to their sense of fashion. While the stylistic manner of this seduction has changed since these ads were first printed, the method is still the same: appeal to weakness, bolster myth, and massage fantasy.

Originally published as "The D Word: Smoke Gets in Your Eyes" on *Design Observer,* March 23, 2016.

## DISCUSSION POINTS

- If the role of advertising is to persuade, does this mean at any cost?
- Is comparing advertising and graphic design a false equivalency?
- Do designers have a responsibility to refuse to work on harmful products?
- How do advertising practitioners exploit the consumer?

# FIVE: INSPIRATION AND DISCOVERIES

*Albert Einstein never thought about the future; he said it came soon enough. Relatively speaking, the future is happening the very second you read this sentence and all the sentences that follow. The future is now, tomorrow, and the next day. In each case we may have an educated idea, but really do not know what is coming next. So it is much more comforting to look at the past-future. The future is pretty clear when seen through a rearview mirror.*

# Visions of the Future

Rather than attempt yet another prognostication, it is safer to look back to see why the future was so exciting and then to reflect upon what those futuristic promises became. Looking back is far more soothing than looking forward. Of course, not even the past always posited a rosy future. There were plenty of real and potential horrors to scare us—utopias turned into dystopias in the blink of an eye or the decree of a ruler. But like Dickens's Ghost of Christmas Yet to Come, somehow, when seen through a nostalgic gauze, we have long believed it is possible to change the course of human events, if only our smartest visionaries put their minds to it.

However, visionaries being only human, they didn't always have 20/20 future vision. They couldn't always get it right. But they often came damn close and presented possibilities that were rooted in the realm of possibility. When those visionaries were artists and designers, they didn't just fantasize— although fantasy is the stock-in-trade of many artists. Rather, working with science and technology, they nudged into the future, or what with certain tweaks became the future.

Space travel, for instance, was seriously anticipated long before there was propulsion. Rockets were imagined prior to theories of aerodynamics. Yet curiously, in addition to the ludicrous predictions, a share of the visions were fairly accurate. Even before the Wright Brothers made their initial leap to the heavens, artist conceptions of airships were not that far off the mark. Of course, it is always funny to see how near or far off some of these contraptions were. Flying saucers have yet to be realized per se, but stealth fighters and bombers are not too far afield from the science fiction precedents.

Yet the visions of the future examined here are not entirely born of science fiction; most derive from science fact and technological reality, transformed by designers (anonymous and known) into actual prototypes that were turned into reality. In the past, various ways of realizing the future were possible. One was "The World of Tomorrow," the name given to the 1939 New York World's Fair that emerged like Oz on a reacclimated ash heap called Flushing Meadows.

"I try to remember how the pastel lighting glowed on Mad Meadow in Flushing: soft greens, orange, yellow, and red; blue moonglow on the great Perisphere and on the ghostly soaring Trylon. I think with a sense of sweetened pain of nights when I sat by Flushing River and saw the World of Tomorrow reflected on its onyx surface, in full color, and upside down," wrote Meyer Berger about the centerpiece of the fair, the ghostly yet futuristic Trylon and Perisphere.

The 1939/40 New York World's Fair—"Fair of the Future," "The World of Tomorrow"—was a masterpiece of showmanship, the epitome of stagecraft. More than a collection of exhibits, it was a wellspring of innovation, sponsored by the most future-minded American corporations (when

America's industry reigned supreme, and would rise even higher). "This Fair of Tomorrow is a promise for the future built with the tools of Today, upon the experience of Yesterday," proclaimed the corporate founders of the Fair.

Consistent with the Fair's precept that "super civilization . . . is based on the swift work of machines, not on the arduous toil of men," the Fair was conceived as a mélange of provocative, often symbolically designed pavilions (some representing a trend in *architecture parlante,* or billboard architecture, in which a building's exterior look revealed its interior purpose—e.g., the Aviation Building was shaped like a dirigible hangar) that were organized into thematic zones covering all aspects of human activity that wed man and machine; Transportation, Production and Distribution, Communications and Business Systems, Community Interest, Government, Food, Medicine and Public Health, and Science and Education.

*Democracity,* the Fair's central theme exhibit, designed by industrial designer Henry Dreyfuss, was an idealized projection of America in 2039, an interdependent network of urban, suburban, and rural areas. Viewed from two moving circular galleries, the visitor had a bird's-eye view of Centeron, a modern, perfectly planned riverside metropolis that could accommodate a million people but, in fact, had no inhabitants because it was used exclusively as the hub of commerce, education, and culture. The mellow yet authoritative voice of the recorded narrator, underscored by music written by William Grant Still and conducted by Andre Kostelanetz, told visitors about a population that lived in commodious high-rises amid suburban garden developments or Pleasantvilles and in light industrial communities and satellite towns called Millvilles, rimmed by fertile and profitable farming zones or sustainable greenbelts, all linked, of course, by modern express highways and parkways. "This is not a vague dream of a life that might be lived in the far future," wrote Robert Kohn, chairman of the Fair's Board of Design, "but one that could be lived tomorrow morning if we willed it so."

*Democracity* was housed in the enormous globe called the Perisphere, a white futuristic temple that also served as the fair's indelible architectural trademark. Designed by Wallace K. Harrison and J. Andre Foulihoux, who had been involved in the design of Rockefeller Center, the Perisphere was 180 feet in diameter and eighteen stories high. The theme center emerged

*"This is not a vague dream of a life that might be lived in the far future," wrote Robert Kohn, chairman of the Fair's Board of Design, "but one that could be lived tomorrow morning if we willed it so."*

after more than one thousand sketches and models. Despite its unique form, it was not without design precedents, including references to the Futurist wellsprings, the Bauhaus and Russian Constructivism.

Each hour more than eight thousand enthusiastic spectators entered the Perisphere through the Trylon, a triangular obelisk 610 feet high, larger than the Washington Monument. Ascending on the two large escalators to a sixty-five-foot-high bridge that led directly into this visionary extravaganza. Six minutes later they would exit down the Helicline, an eighteen-foot-wide ramp with a stainless steel underbelly.

No sales pitch for the future was as persuasive as the one extolled in *Democracity*. Laid before Mr. and Mrs. Average American in all its colorful splendor was the grandest World of Tomorrow—and it was entirely real. Equivalent to more than 370 city blocks, it included more than 200 modern and modernistic buildings curiously laid out according to a nineteenth-century *beaux-arts rond-point* system of radiating streets and fanlike segments extending like spokes from a central hub.

The future was conceived and constructed by industrial designers, among them Raymond Loewy, Walter Dorwin Teague, Henry Dreyfuss, Donald Desky, Egmond Arens, Russell Wright, Gilbert Rohde, and Norman Bel Geddes. These were industry's predominant form-givers whose "faith was . . . based on moral conviction," wrote historian Francis V. O'Connor, "that the public good was to be attained by the universal adoption of a certain rightness of form in all matters from the design of cities to the styling of pencil sharpeners." They designed the lighting stanchions and sculptural fixtures. Most of the kinetic exhibits were also imaginatively designed by proponents of the new Streamline aesthetic.

Loewy conceived of the Chrysler Corporation and Transportation exhibits; Teague, who was also a skilled but pedestrian commercial artist, designed seven exhibits, including those for Kodak, U.S. Steel, Consolidated Edison, Dupont, National Cash Register, and Ford; Desky applied Surrealism to the Communications exhibit, and Russell Wright did likewise for Food. Of all these, however, the most memorable was the brainchild of a one-time scenic designer, Norman Bel Geddes. His theatrical extravaganza for General Motors, called *Futurama*, was housed in architect Alfred Kahn's seven-square-acre Streamline monument, and was the most ambitious and visionary multimedia educational entertainment built for any World's Fair.

The future was, however, a most aggressively merchandised event. Among the thousands of souvenirs were toys and games, ranging from kazoos to paint sets, all emblazoned or molded in the shape of the Trylon and Perisphere.

The efforts of the World's Fair's planners must not be dismissed as a vain effort to predict the future. In fact, many significant inventions and products, from television to fluorescent lights to Kodachrome film, were introduced there. It was a colorful, though fleeting, beacon of hope that signaled an end to the Great Depression and the beginning of World War II. Under the sign of the Trylon and Perisphere, the Fair left fond memories of the future and a promise of all the futures to come once World War II was won.

Originally published in *Print* magazine, Fall 2017.

# DISCUSSION POINTS

- What can be learned from looking back at the future?
- Is nostalgia a constructive attribute in design?
- Does predicting the future require understanding the past?
- Do designers have the ability to predict the future?

*When Fritz Lang directed the landmark Futurist film* Metropolis *in 1927, the Great War had devastated Europe, the Machine Age was revving up, and dreaming without limit was in vogue: the future had endless possibilities for human and machine.*

# Nostalgia for Futures Past

The future was as astonishing, dynamic, and as startling as it was frightening. With the right science anything was possible, including spandex and Lycra.

Robots, not cockroaches, were poised to inherit the earth—as slaves. The idea was to make objects mechanical enough to do our drudgery, as in the case of a robotic garbage disposal, but not rule our lives.

Of course, robots could also be sinister. Despite the steel diaper, the robot from *The Day the Earth Stood Still* suggests that with one false move, the recipient of his death ray will never see the future.

Our past-future was bound to the notion that chemistry and technology would ultimately have a beneficial outcome for our planet. Robbie the Robot was almost human, but keep him away from my sister.

In Woody Allen's *Sleeper*, robots were perfect slaves that could be satisfied and kept in line by a few strokes of the pleasure-emitting orb. In the future, sex was indeed a solitary act. The future was also about going to worlds only visited in the imagination. Marie-Georges-Jean Méliès's *A Trip to the Moon* (Le voyage dans la Lune), made in 1902, addressed the conquering of the planets through manned space vehicles. Earlier in the nineteenth century, airplanes were envisioned, and the next logical step was a rocket to the moon. Take that, Mr. Man in the Moon.

And so it came to pass, fifty years later, that the moon was colonized, if only in the imagination of advertising artists.

Nowhere was the future better envisioned than in the World's Fairs around the world. Nowhere was the future better realized than these fairs. The engineering brilliance of Gustav Eiffel was realized as the arch to the 1889 World's Fair. Today it continues to stand as a monument to progress.

The original Ferris wheel was designed and constructed by George Washington Gale Ferris Jr. as a landmark for the 1893 World's Columbian Exposition in Chicago. Each car was as large as a subway tram.

The 1939 New York World's Fair, called "The World of Tomorrow," was conceived and designed by industrial designers, the likes of which the world had not seen—Raymond Loewy, Norman Bel Geddes, Walter Dorwin Teague, Henry Dreyfuss, and more. They created structures that were both Oz-like in their fantasy and futuristic in their vision of the post-mechanical age.

They seem to have been influenced by Lang's *Metropolis* insofar as they saw urban life as an interconnected system of road- and skyways that relied on automobiles and autogyros for transportation.

World's Fairs continued to be showcases for the future. At the 1963 New York Fair, the future offered push-button phones, video telephones, and the Unisphere, representing peace and freedom.

The future would be just another epoch, if not for the computer, starting with the huge UNIVAC, evolving to the IBM mainframes and ultimately the desktop. The future had to run on what would later be called artificial intelligence. Without computers, human and alien cultures could not survive.

Computers, like wireless radios before, became the province of future geeks, like Steve Jobs and Steve "Woz" Wozniak, who were playing with the prototype for the Apple.

The result was the Apple II, which evolved into the Macintosh. The Macintosh 128K was announced to the press in October 1983, followed by an eighteen-page brochure included with various magazines in December, and introduced by the now famous $1.5 million Ridley Scott television commercial, "1984." Big Brother was named Steve Jobs.

The future was full of science fiction. Some of it was metaphor for the Cold War, as in aliens come to invade. Science fiction was a form of propaganda for good and evil—democracy and dictatorship. The future was full of mutant beings because we played with the wrong futuristic materials.

But Stanley Kubrick's *2001* was a cautionary tale about humanity's overreliance on computers . . . and artificial intelligence. The future has come full circle. Humans were just babes in the woods when it came to predicting what's next.

---

Adapted from a lecture delivered by the author in 2014.

# DISCUSSION POINTS

- How is design for the future designed?

- Is there a language of the future?

- Is science fiction a viable vision of the future?

- Is there a typeface that says "future"?

*Ever since seeing* Fantastic Voyage, *the 1966 science fiction film about a crew of biologists atomically miniaturized to fit into a microbe-sized submarine sailing perilously through the human bloodstream, encountering dangers like parasites and immune system defenses along the way, I've fantasized that tiny homunculi actually control our bodies. And our bodies are really huge factories.*

# Man as Industrial Palace

I admit thinking of the self as a metaphoric factory is a naively comforting way to make sense of the human condition, akin to my childhood belief that real little people were actually performing in my TV set. Yet little did I know until now that someone far more learned and obsessive than I, a German scientist, gynecologist, and author named Fritz Kahn (1888–1968), not only developed this idea in the 1920s but created a copyrighted graphic system that visually codified the metaphoric notion of man as machine, which he introduced to the world in a comical diagrammatic poster titled "Man as Industrial Palace" (1926). Comic artwork aside, Kahn was quite serious.

*. . . [Kahn] was similarly concerned with taking the mystery out of the miracle of life by presenting it in words and pictures almost everyone could comprehend.*

The poster, a cutaway schematic of a human form, reveals a complex industrial apparatus housed in numerous compartments analogous to bodily organs and cellular functions. In these rooms, dozens of presumably skilled homunculi (some wearing business suits) are controlling all the operations as though it were a normal day at the industrial park. But if you've never seen the original, which is included as full-size pull-out reproduction in a new, profusely illustrated biographical monograph, *Fritz Kahn: Man Machine* by Uta and Thilo von Debschitz, and on their website http://www.fritz-kahn.com/, you may have seen many imitations over the past decades. Unbeknownst to me, Kahn was the master of such visualization. I still vividly recall an iconic version from 1950s commercials advertising Bufferin (which included the indelible image of a sledgehammer in the head representing a pounding headache).

In Kahn's universe the human body was more fascinating than the facile attempts of Bufferin's ad agency to simplify a complex medical problem. But he was similarly concerned with taking the mystery out of the miracle of life by presenting it in words and pictures almost everyone could comprehend. "The cell state is a republic under the hereditary hegemony of the mind's aristocracy," he wrote. "Its economic system is a strict communism." No wonder his books were placed on the Nazi list of "harmful and unwanted writings" and publicly burned. His medical license was revoked and he was forced to emigrate first to Palestine, then Paris until the occupation. Next he went to Spain. Then, thanks to Albert Einstein's intervention, he ultimately was granted a special visa to the United States. Along the way an unscrupulous German publisher infringed on his copyright by republishing

*…these are milestones of visualization, making complex things easy to understand (which is a daily struggle of each communication designer, or at least should be).*

Kahn's five-volume opus, *Das Leben Des Menschen* (1922–1931), without obtaining permission or giving credit. Around ten years after the war, he regained copyright and began affixing the FK monogram to every piece issued by his firm.

Kahn's poster wittily reveals the left and right top of the brain, where thinking occurs. It is there that studious homunculi are reading, drawing, and discussing. The eye is a large bellows camera (although I don't see a darkroom, so it must prefigure the Polaroid instant camera). As a concrete example of how the body functions, food is consumed and shown traveling down into the bowels of the machine, where less formally dressed workers break it down into sugars and starches and other components that are conveyed along a mechanical production line to other rooms. Although one would not want to be operated on by a surgeon who learned anatomy lessons this way, the visualizations are decidedly enlightening.

Kahn was not a skilled writer or artist, but he hired many others to follow his lead. According to Thilo von Debschitz, a graphic designer (Uta, a writer, studied architecture) in an email, Kahn employed "an enormous bandwidth of styles (including Dadaism, Photo collage, Comic, Surrealism, etc.)." Kahn was also a master at making analogies, comparing an ear with a car or a birds' feather with railroad tracks, all meant to explain phenomena while triggering imagination. "For me as a designer," adds von Debschitz, "these are milestones of visualization, making complex things easy to understand (which is a daily struggle of each communication designer, or at least should be). Therefore, there is big relevance in his work for today. Not only in terms of design, but in terms of communication at all, such as teaching science."

The Industrial Palace poster may be Kahn's most emblematic work, but it is not the only piece of note in his oeuvre. He embraced the ideas of modernism, and his followers included Herbert Bayer and Walter Gropius of the Bauhaus. He also used new technologies as visualization tools for explaining themes as diverse as sight and smell. One of his most illuminating diagrams was "What Goes On in Our Heads When We See a Car and Say 'Car.'" It is a complex orchestration of functions starting with the eye, imprinting a message on a conveyor of film that leads to a projection booth, inhabited by a lab-coat-clad projectionist homunculus projecting a photo of the car onto a screen that says "car." The message is then broadcast to a pipe-organ that toots out the word "Car." If only it really worked this way, life would be so much easier to understand.

As I flipped through the beautiful Fritz Kahn monograph, I happened upon an image titled "Fairytale journey along the bloodstream," with a homunculus surfing on a platelet into a glandular cavity. It occurred to me that this drawing could have been the basis for *Fantastic Voyage*, and I thought maybe this way of thinking about life may not be so naïve after all.

Originally published as the introduction in *Fritz Kahn: Infographics Pioneer* by Uta von Debschitz and Thilo von Debschitz (Los Angeles: TASCHEN America, 2013).

# DISCUSSION POINTS

- What is the metaphor(s) that Kahn is attempting to depict?
- Do you think of the body as a machine?
- Can a machine be thought of in human terms?
- Why are anthropomorphized machines so fascinating to create?

# Be Careful What You Dream For

I used to daydream a lot about inventing things that were never realized, like an interactive television where you could stick your hand through the top of the set and move the characters around or remove them at will. It was one of many crazy daydreams, some of which turned into real nightmares.

But in the early 1960s, when I was twelve years old, over a decade before the widespread commercial use of telephone answering devices and long before social media barged into everyone's private life, I foresaw real possibilities for these and other existential, life-enhancing inventions. My concern was not for the betterment of mankind. Rather, mine were egoistical, selfish, and narcissistic reasons that nonetheless presaged how many current inventions are now used.

I wasn't the first to contemplate telephone answering machines (apparently, the prototype emerged from Bell Labs in 1930), but I didn't know that when I conceived mine. My version was born of personal need. My dad refused what I considered a perfectly reasonable request to pay a monthly fee for what was then known as an answering "service" (an operator who would answer your phone and take messages). When I was twelve, newly interested in girls (although unrequited), I used to fret that when I was away from home I'd miss the all-important call from the girl (whoever she might be), who I fantasized about as becoming my steady girlfriend. Unable to reach me on the phone, she would become discouraged and/or forget to call back. I was an insecure kid. I believed when I was not home to answer the phone I was missing out on everything that would make life more fulfilling. If only a machine were invented, I thought, that would pick up the phone, tell the caller I was off doing something important, and record a message.

I imagined designing a contraption that would accomplish this very task. Yet, without the fundamentals of electrical engineering (I skipped shop in junior high), I was unable to make my dream come true. My grandma was fond of saying, "If you wait long enough, *dahlink*, someone smarter than you will figure everything out." Lo and behold, she was right. By the time I was nineteen or so, "answer-matic" phones were announced, and two or three years later magnetic tape machines were comparatively affordable. I bought a Panasonic, plugged it in, and my dream came true. But a new problem arose: The red blinking light, indicating a precious message was waiting, rarely blinked. That was when I realized it was actually better *not* to have an answering device. Without one I could at least fantasize that someone had called me. With it, I knew that not a soul (especially that extra-special someone) had called. I'm older and less insecure than in those days, but no less addicted to the machine source of self-esteem. I still look at the blinking light for solace and validation. Designers and engineers have done wonders in wiring us up so that we're never untethered from the phone or other device, but the emotional price is high.

I also had an idea the prefigured the rise of social media. It was not Facebook or Twitter per se, but it was a telepathic means to enable people to perhaps satisfy another persistent need: to know for a fact what others really thought of them at any given time.

The idea went like this: A transmitter (you) would send out a kind of mind-wave impulse that would be received by a receiver (me). The transmitter would indicate whether he or she loved, liked, or disliked the receiver. At the end of the day, or at any convenient time, the receiver would review all the messages, learning how the people with whom he or she interacted felt. I conceived that the body, acting like a dispenser, would spit out the results via paper. Crazy, right? But what are Twitter's and Facebook's "like" indicators if not my concept transformed from telepathic to digital technology? And what are today's message-making devices but high-tech ways to satisfy the primal and/or neurotic need to be the center of attention?

If I had the right kind of smarts, "I coulda been an inventor, I coulda been somebody!" (with apologies to Marlon Brando in *On the Waterfront*). My ideas, born of narcissism, were made real and monetized by others who were, as Grandma said, "smarter" than me. What I fantasized about inventing turned into the source of twenty-first-century obsessions. "Fantasy abandoned by reason produces impossible monsters," wrote Francisco Goya in his *Los Caprichos*, and my answering and social media concepts are those monsters, are they not?

———————————

Originally published as "Watch Out What You Day-Dream For" in *Design Observer*, April 25, 2019.

# DISCUSSION POINTS

- Do you have vivid fantasies about inventing something new?

- If you were to invent a design product, how would you market and promote it?

- As a creative person, is it possible to monetize your ideas?

- What are some ideas that you dream about making?

*Here is a familiar scene. Awestruck children longingly—and raptly—peering into a toy store window filled with a cornucopia of commercial playthings, Each aspiring to possess the doll, train, bike, or any of thousands of child-targeted merchandise created for their enjoyment. For kids (and some adults too), toys trigger an irrepressible urge to have, hold, and consume. Not just simple diversions, toys are motivators; toys are rewards; toys are business. This essay looks at the simple design of toys that triggered play, inspiration, and creativity.*

# Toy Story

In the 1950s, an afternoon TV game show aired where kid contestants were allotted five minutes to scarf up as many toys as their small arms and hands could carry off (whatever they could not hold had to be left behind). The sight of such rampant avariciousness was at once amusing (like watching someone herd chickens in a pen), yet disturbing (like watching madness of the mind). Imagine what it feels like to be let loose for five minutes in heaven (or elsewhere)—you might never recover from the consequences of such freedom. When the buzzer rang, signaling the time limit had been reached, the lucky prizewinners proudly displayed their booty for the audience to admire (triggering, of course, their own desire to purchase them). Decades later, Nickelodeon's Super Toy Run applied the same psychology to a higher, more rapturous extreme, with the chosen ones accelerating down aisles filling carts with the latest kid-sumables. "It turned even the 'sweetest' most 'adorable' child into creatures so inhuman in their avaris," noted a blogger on the toy site the Modern Day Pirates, "they made Gangis Kahn look like Gandi [sic]."

*Toys fulfill many a child's natural and usually harmless desires to play and fiddle, but there is nothing innocent about toy advertisements.*

I was never lucky enough to be selected for that 1950s show—though not from lack of trying—but I experienced my own version of this particular heaven on earth. As compensation for enduring a torturous tonsil removal operation, I was allowed to select three toys from the legendary Rappaport's Toy Bazaar, located for ninety years at Third Avenue near Seventy-ninth Street in Manhattan—the same store that, until it closed in 1981, wrapped its wares in polka-dot paper (which was the inspiration for Stuart Davis's 1951 painting *Rapt at Rappaport's*). My mom and dad knew the co-owner, Harold Ostrover, who, in the spirit of the TV show, jokingly told me I had five minutes to decide what I wanted from the massive shelves filled with play toy bounty. I thought he was serious, so I made a mad dash, and as my heart pumped and adrenaline surged, I recalled the dozens of Saturday-morning commercials for the latest name-brand toys and tie-ins and all the ads for them in *Life*, *Look*, and other magazines. My choices were exclusively based on what the top ten toys were at the moment and the kind of status they would bring among my community of envious friends. Product status derived from advertising campaigns—such was the power of propaganda to direct behavior, even when it came to toys.

Toys fulfill many a child's natural and usually harmless desires to play and fiddle, but there is nothing innocent about toy *advertisements*. They are gateways to a life of consumption, in this case products designed to profit their maker even when camouflaged as educational. Yes, it's true that some toys are educational, and all toys play an important role in a child's life. During those thrilling days of yesteryear, more were tacitly promoted as positive developmental tools. Take the story in the *Ladies' Home Journal* for

July 1916 titled "Teaching a Child Resourcefulness": "Every normal child is most happy when he is 'making' something or 'pretending' some situation even though there may be no visible result that harmonizes with the thought in the little mind," wrote Mildred Austin Shinn, adding that "little ones" derive more satisfaction from making playthings from materials found in the home.

This may be true, but children also like getting things that are already designed, fabricated, and branded—playthings that other children have or aspire to be given that express life's privileges and benefits of wealth, race, or ethnicity. Competitive buying and owning is not just an adult syndrome—it starts with kids.

Toys may be objects of joy, yet children are not the paying customer. *Pic* magazine warned in 1941: "Although there have been great strides in the improvement of toys . . . the average parent still buys the toy that catches his own eye, and gives little effect, good or bad, on the child for whom it is intended." In the story, cleverly subtitled "Your Youngster's Future Depends Upon the Present," the Toy Guidance Council notes that not all educational toys are attractive and may be easily ignored by the child. A toy should be selected commensurate with the child's "natural aptitudes." A child, it says, "can be retarded considerably by being forced to play with toys which no longer interest it." Certain toys can confuse a child and make them feel inferior. So the most important quality for a toy is that it "encourage group activity, that [it] teach your little one to get along with other children." In addition to fun, toys should have "an actual everyday experience or imitation of adults."

In the early years of mass media, toy advertising was not as calculated as it later became, in part because toys were actually more educational. Meccano building model systems, created in 1898 by Englishman Frank Hornby, were among the most frequent advertisers. But the first major American toy advertiser was its American doppelganger, Erector (later bought by Meccano). Inducted into the National Toy Hall of Fame in 1998, the classic Erector Set, conceived by A. C. Gilbert, was made of metal girders and mechanical components, held together by little grub screws. "Businessmen and industrial psychologists hailed the toy that put play to

*You'd think that bicycles would be gender neutral, but in 1919, Haverford Cycle Co. pitched its Black Beauty to boys only.*

work and encouraged children's 'constructive instincts,'" notes the National Museum of Play website. Through a national campaign in the *Saturday Evening Post* and *Popular Mechanics*, the Erector Set premiered in 1913. The ads were aimed at boys, not girls. Launched around same time as the introduction of Lincoln Logs and Tinkertoys, Erector Sets introduced boys to engineering and the structural principles of modern skyscrapers. Expanded kits with electric motors empowered users to build trains, steam shovels, Ferris wheels, and Zeppelins.

Erector set the tone for toy advertisements of various "imitative" toys. The .22 caliber repeating Remington Rifle and Winchester ("Oh, J-I-M-M-Y, come on over, we're goin' shootin'!") and Stevens ("Hitting the Bullseye since 1864") actually shot real bullets, while the King, Sterling, and Daisy Air Rifles only shot air and BBs, although Daisy's ad said "Every healthy, natural, boyish boy wants and needs a gun"—even one with a bayonet. Guns were frequently sold (Milton Bradley marketed a machine gun called "Big Dick" that fired wooden bullets—$3.00), but there were safer play options. In magazines like *Boys' Life* (published for the Boy Scouts), Ives Toys and Lionel sold electric train sets ("ask Dad for this train"). There was the Flexible Flyer sled, touted as fast and sturdy. In addition, table tennis, fortune-telling games, and a genuine ($1.50) Indian wigwam ("Just the thing for the Boys"). Boys could also "Own a Speedy Car," learn how to build and fly three-foot-long model war aeroplanes, and "Build Real Forts" with Richter's Anchor Blocks. Small space ads sold things like Zimmerman's Flying Machine, "a marvel of simplicity," a "scientifically" designed kite that "any boy or girl could fly." With Skudder Car, "every boy and girl in the block envies the youngster who owns one." And girls alone were targeted with Dolly's Home ("A Fairy-tale come true!"). Speaking of Dolly, those were highly prized, like the famous "Mary Jane" ("There's nothing you could give a little girl that she'd love so much as Mary Jane—nothing she'd hug so close to her heart").

You'd think that bicycles would be gender neutral, but in 1919, Haverford Cycle Co. pitched its Black Beauty to boys only. Although wagons, like the Sheboygan Speedster and scooters, were more universal, and home playgrounds and swing sets were for girls and boys. As were the Toy Tinkers Company's famous Tinkertoys, which were artfully designed in a somewhat avant-garde manner.

Many toys did indeed re-create the adult experience. For girls' kitchen miniatures, "all the fun of a cabinet 'Just Like Mother's'" gave little girls some homemaking experience.

In the 1930s, toys were often sold or given away as premiums for buying other products, such as Wheaties, Ralston, and Quaker cereals. Comic characters lent their personas to toys as well—Dick Tracy sold aviation equipment. As war was looming in Europe, some toys took on a military flavor, including Comet airplane models. Still, most of the toy-making materials were limited because of wartime restrictions, so throughout the war neither toy manufacture or advertising was a high priority. In the postwar normality, dolls, magic kits, and board games made a comeback. Innovation—sort of—was on the rise as well, including the Kangru-Springshu, a pair of skates that instead of wheels had tough springs for jumping and running.

The late 1940s and early '50s were times for saving fun in specially made banks, building structures with Playskool building blocks, taking photographs with Roy Rogers's "pow'ful" box camera, or looking in neighbor's windows with his branded binoculars. New materials were coming into the world with iconic brands in tow. Hasbro's Mr. and Mrs. Potato Head planted their roots in 1954 as one of the company's top ten toys. Silly Putty was advertised in 1958 for the first time. Slinky made its first appearance in 1957. The technology was possible for an electric doll that could walk like Effanbee's Norma. By 1955, Mickey Mouse ears came into the vernacular, along with dozens of other branded clothing/costumes, like Davy Crockett frontier kidswear and Roy Rogers's one- and two-gun holsters and pistols. By the 1960s, toys and the ads marketing them became more sophisticated in design and content. A 1962 ad for Mattel showed children of color with dolls of the same skin. Another Mattel advancement was the "Cheerful Tearful" doll, conceived like any adult ad. A 1967 ad for Lego, with the headline "Lego, the toy they won't be tired of by Dec 26th," not only looked adult but was as smart as any "Big Idea" ad for adult products (the tag line lived up to the promise "Lego. . . The thoughtful toy"). As the years rolled on, so did the advertisements for life-lesson products like Barbie, Midget Mustang, *Julia* (the first TV series with an African American star), and Signature Junior electric portable sewing machine. Fisher-Price Sesame Street products and others were obviously aimed at adults who had become familiar with the advertising industry's Creative Revolution's visual language.

---

Previously unpublished.

## DISCUSSION POINTS

- What are or were some of your favorite toys and why?

- Did toys trigger a creative impulse that made you want to design things?

- How have toys changed from the early twentieth century to the early twenty-first century?

- Are toys made only for children?

*Our evolutionary kissing cousin, the monkey, has been a staple of graphic wit and visual commentary as far back as . . . well, nobody knows exactly. But in both Eastern and Western art and design, monkeys—along with apes, gorillas, and other primates— have evolved over the millennia from simple simians into complex symbolic surrogates of you and me. This essay monkeys around with visual language.*

# Anthro-pomorphic Simians

Anthropomorphism dates back to at least ancient Egypt, when animal heads were artfully grafted atop human torsos for celebratory and satirical purposes. Certain gods were holistically portrayed as *manimals*, part us and part them. Egyptian slaves also made anthropomorphized depictions of their overseers (since less roundabout sardonic likenesses would have been punishable by torture and death).

Anthropomorphism ultimately became the most ubiquitous genre of visual comic art, from J. J. Grandville's nineteenth-century satiric menageries to Walt Disney's twentieth-century licensing zoos, filled with English-speaking cartoon animals. Monkeys are kings of the graphic jungle, although they can also play the role of court jester. Their antic behavior, combined with their resemblance to humans, has made them ripe for all kinds of political satire, cultural comedy, and racial manipulation. Since they slip so easily into human clothing, monkeys can easily be made to embody our best and worst traits. Even our vernacular is replete with simian allusions: "making a monkey out of me," "going ape," "monkey business," "monkey suit," "monkey on my back."

During the Victorian era, the Irish were caricatured as apelike, and African Americans have long been targets of similar attacks—shamefully, in as high-profile an outlet as the *New York Post*, as recently as 2009. But historically, monkeys haven't only been trotted out for racist effect. The late-nineteenth-century British cartoonist Arthur H. Marks took "Ape" as his nom de crayon because he aped his subject's characteristics. In 1871, for obvious reasons, Charles Darwin was portrayed as an ape in the satiric journal *The Wasp*. Later, *L'Assiette au Beurre* ridiculed French judges as chimps blindly following idiotic decrees. In the same magazine, well-dressed cartoon monkeys represent the fools in commentaries on the *comédie humaine*. More recently, there have been the evil monkeys of Oz and *Family Guy*, the Jeeves-like Mr. Teeny on *The Simpsons*, and the brawny bit-drawn Donkey Kong—all shards of an uncanny mirror. Monkeys are on artists' and designers' minds (and backs) more than you'd imagine. To find out just how much, you could send out a poll via SurveyMonkey on Mailchimp. I think you'd find the results are bananas.

Originally published in *Print* magazine, April 2012.

## DISCUSSION POINTS

- What is the role of anthropomorphism in contemporary art and design?
- Are these depictions unfair to either or both humans and animals?
- Can humans relate better to humanized animals?
- What is the most familiar anthropomorphic character and why?

*Not to wax nostalgic about letterheads, but the logo and typography printed prominently on a fine sheet of bond paper, printed offset or letterpress, embodies authority, which email messages do not (unless they include PDF attachments, which are not real letterheads). Letterheads are like the official wax seals—the signet rings of yore—and there is nothing comparable in the texting or email worlds (not even red flags or exclamation points).*

# The Letterhead: Necessity or Accessory?

To receive a physical letterhead is an entirely different experience that moves one in ways that digital correspondence, even containing emojis, cannot achieve. Consider receiving a letter from the president of the United States (as I have, though not to brag, on a couple of occasions). Which is more pleasurable: opening an envelope that includes a note with the embossed presidential seal, or scrolling through an email with an emoticon? There's just no comparison.

Yet paper letterhead usage is on the decline. Designers continue to design them, but not with the frequency or abundance of even ten years ago, when letterhead/envelope/business card competitions were judged and documented in hefty books and professional magazines. The average twentieth-century business used to send hundreds of personally typed letters daily. Today, the business card usually contains an email address and URL, bypassing the need for paper letters entirely. More than ever, we care about saving the planet's resources through paperless offices. Woe be the letterhead.

Still, letterheads have as important a role in commercial life as they ever did. They still demand attention. They still serve the prestige of the company or institution for which they stand. They still imply legitimacy. And, although this is not an immediate benefit, they are evidence of design history, fashion, and trends.

"When an unknown monastic scribe in Byzantium started one of his manuscripts with an enlarged letter and began to embellish this letter with color and ornamentation, the first seedling of the modern letterhead was planted," wrote Ernst Lehner in *The Letterhead: History and Progress* (Museum Books, 1955).

Although letterheads could have come from those seedlings, as Lehner asserts, they are also related to the impressions pressed into sealing substances. During the early nineteenth century, engravings were printed atop sheets of otherwise blank paper—some were quite large, and all were brands of sorts. But even earlier, in the late eighteenth century, decorative illustration became smaller and moved up to the top to leave more room and slowly assumed the appearance of the familiar letterhead. A certain amount of excess returned during the late nineteenth century, when "the butcher, the baker and the candlestick maker of yesteryear were trying their best to use decent business paper for their bills and correspondence," wrote Lehner, referring to the rise in letterheads and billheads demanded by newly minted

*Letterheads were obnoxiously ornate
and overcooked, not unlike ostentatious
Greco-Roman revivalist architecture when
"industrialists and business men started
to believe that the letterheads of their firms
were the most fertile ground."*

merchants and manufacturers. The letterhead grew directly from flyers that announced small businesses' wares and services. This form was also used for the invoice, which gave way to the letterhead/billhead, which allowed for detailed correspondence and a tally of what the customer owed.

The rise of commerce spawned the need among businesses in neighboring localities to know how each conducted business. So a merchants' newsletter was conceived, which evolved into the classic newspaper with a typographic nameplate or masthead. It is this typographic/illustrative accoutrement that influenced the look of the letterhead; it is also where Lehner chides the so-called "art printers" devoted to social and business stationery from the late nineteenth and early twentieth centuries for unleashing "a deluge of commercialized tastelessness."

Letterheads were obnoxiously ornate and overcooked, not unlike ostentatious Greco-Roman revivalist architecture when "industrialists and business men started to believe that the letterheads of their firms were the most fertile ground," Lehner contemptuously writes, and "kowtowing to their personal vanity and the right space to show themselves how big and important they are."

During this early stage of letterheads, there was indeed a degeneration of type: "inferior and bizarre letters were cast for the sake of being different."

Despite the excessive use of decorative swirls and flourishes weaving through, above, and below engravings of factory complexes or cuts of tools and machines, these letterheads have an American tenacity. But letterhead standards fluctuated wildly. Design calmed down somewhat once twentieth-century modernity emerged, and later it found newer excesses too. Lehner took issue with "Sloppy appearance and Zoot-suitism," which he attacked "as both bad policy for business representative and paper alike."

The examples in his book were drawn from many of the most illustrious modern designers of the early to mid-1950s, including Ladislav Sutnar and Lester Beall. The minimalism that ensued after the Bauhaus and its adherents got hold of this genre led to very rationally beautiful designs. Simultaneously, however, the now-kitschy versions filled with vintage trade characters and novelty type still were produced.

Lehner took his tough critical stance against excess because "Letterheads are not here today and gone tomorrow." However, if he were still alive he'd see that globalization, mergers and acquisitions, and universal branding have made a category of letterhead that is distinguishable but the same, and do often change from today to tomorrow.

---

Originally published in *Print* magazine, Fall 2016.

# DISCUSSION POINTS

- What is the "trick" to designing a successful letterhead?

- With email and messaging, is it still important to have letterheads?

- Are there substantive differences between pre- and post-digital letterheads?

- Letterheads are printed on paper. How important is the quality of paper and printing to the entire process?

# The Roots of Design

According to the Department of Labor Statistics, hair design is big business. According to my uneducated guess, it is a billion-dollar industry, between wigs, toupees, and all manner of stylists, styling products, and styling photos shot to sell pomades, gels, shampoos, nets, and more. No wonder, according to literature and the Bible too, many characters are defined by their hair.

My hair, hair, hair, hair, hair, hair, hair
Flow it, show it
Long as God can grow it
My hair[1]

---

[1] *Hair* original Broadway cast performance of "Hair," written by Galt MacDermot, Gerome Ragni, and James Rado, released January 1, 1968.

You could say that my life has been one bad hair day. From the get-go, my hair has been a divisive issue. When I was a five-month-old baby, my mother insisted that I wear an adorable shock of hair on my noggin like a cockatiel's crest. That presumably innocent touch of hair flair, perhaps an homage to *Our Gang*'s Carl "Alfalfa" Switzer, who wore a famously pomade-waxed cowlick (which he called "my personality"), sealed my fate as a hair-fixated neurotic. I had the mini-plume for a year, until Mom, who changed her own style and color every couple of months, decided it was no longer *au courant*, so she toyed with the idea of letting my hair grow into a Buster Brown cut. My dad, however, put his foot down and insisted Buster Brown was not the right persona for *his* son, and took me, when I was about two and a half, to get my first store-bought haircut.

First haircuts are often traumatic . . . for mothers who routinely save their kid's fallen locks for posterity along with the first bib, rattle, and bronzed baby shoes. Yet speaking of trauma, barber shops in Manhattan were rarely designed to accommodate the psychological consequences of small children under the scissor. These shops were as scary as a doctor's office—but at least pediatricians used child psychology to trick their victims into acquiescence. For me, barbers were much more menacing! Mine could have passed for Edward Scissorhands, but he was no Johnny Depp. Taped to his mirror were dozens of photos of his young clientele at the moment of the initial cut in various stages of hysterics (I made it to the wall of dishonor). That first cut, during which I was being shorn like a lamb, resulted in a lot of tears. To stop my residual whimpering, I received a piece of candy (and I'm still convinced barbers and dentists were in cahoots, for after a few haircuts the cavities emerged).

Hair design has always been important sign, symbol, and mark of status. Growing up in the 1950s and '60s, hair suggested many things, including social class, cultural attitude, and aesthetic preference. From ages five to eight, more or less, I wore the all-American crew and butch cuts with the top glued upward. Crews were the favorite of jar-head athletes—and required little maintenance. But over the next couple of years, as I slowly freed myself from my parents' grip, I began a coif rebellion. By nine or ten I went the greaser route, like Elvis. I started with Vitalis, graduated to Brylcreem

*Growing up in the 1950s and '60s, hair suggested many things, including social class, cultural attitude, and aesthetic preference.*

("a little dab'l do ya"), and by eleven I had a full-fledged pompadour in the front with classic duck's ass in the back, held together by a green lacquer product known among the knowing as "elephant snot." For JDs and wannabe delinquents who cultivated this look, the emerald goo (like glue) would harden the hair in place for a few hours, impervious to any natural elements. But when it melted, what a mess.

My mom hated the pompadour look. "You look unsavory," she'd say. This was supported by the other mothers in Stuy Town, New York, where we lived, who wouldn't allow their kids to play with the local hood. When Elvis went into the army, the pompadour and DA (duck's ass) went south, so I tried a middle ground—not short, not long—with a part on the left and a slight bang in the front. Everyone seemed happy with my choice, even me. Until the Beatles.

I recall when my mom nervously sneered, "I hope you never wear your hair like those . . ." (I think she meant mop tops.) But that was all the excuse I needed to go mod. In came the fringe and bangs (like Moe of the Three Stooges), and as their hair grew out, so did mine. The longer it got, the more frustrated and abusive my mom became. "I hope you go bald, like your father," she harangued, insulting both me and my dad (who eventually got a hair transplant). Jeez, it's only hair, I thought. But as the 1960s wore on, she'd berate my hair, as though it were an ugly wild animal I brought home. But me being me, I let it grow and grow and grow some more until it was all the way down my back.

She wasn't wrong. My excessively long hair was not the most pleasing of my various features. But it was my design, my signature, and, as Alfalfa said, my personality. Paradoxically, Mom won in the end. By age twenty, my dad's genes showed up on my shower stall floor. By twenty-six, it was clear that not even Hair Club for Men could save me. I was losing my personality at a rapid pace, forced to get regular haircuts or look like Benjamin Franklin. I don't know which was more traumatic, the first haircut or the balding. Finally, at around forty-five, I had no choice but to shave it all off, secure only in the knowledge that people like Billy Joel and Michael Stipe were bald too. Shortly after it was all gone, I was visiting my parents. My mom said ruefully, "What a shame, you had such beautiful hair, would you like me to buy you a toupee?" Thanks, Mom!

Originally published as "HAIR: A Design Problem" on *Design Observer*, February 13, 2019.

# DISCUSSION POINTS

- What is so important about a hairstyle?
- Hair styling is considered design. Is it?
- Is hair a stylistic marker of an era?
- If hair is so important, what does baldness say?

# Curse of the "D" Word

Do you make things look nice? Do you spend more time worrying about nuance and aesthetics than substance and meaning? Do you fiddle with style while ignoring the big picture? If your answers are yes, yes, or yes, then you are a decorator.

Being a decorator is not how graphic designers necessarily want to perceive themselves. But what's the big deal? Is anything fundamentally wrong with being a decorator? Although Adolf Loos, an architect, proclaimed ornament as a sin in his essay, "Ornament and Crime," an attack on late-nineteenth-century art nouveau, in truth decoration and ornamentation are no more sinful than purity is supremely virtuous.

Take for example the psychedelic style of the late 1960s that was smothered in flamboyant ornamentation (indeed, much of it borrowed from Loos's dreaded art nouveau). Nonetheless, it was a revolutionary graphic language used as a code for a revolutionary generation—which is exactly the same role art nouveau played seventy years earlier with its vituperative rejection of antiquated nineteenth-century academic verities. Likewise, psychedelia's immediate forerunner, Push Pin Studios, from the late 1950s through the 1970s, was known for reprising passé decorative conceits. In the context of the times, it was a purposeful and strategic alternative to the purist Swiss style that evolved into drab corporate modernism, which had rejected decoration (and eclectic quirkiness) in favor of bland Helvetica. In their view, content and meaning were not sacrificed but rather illuminated and made more appealing.

Anti-decorative ideological fervor to the contrary, decoration is not inherently good or bad. While frequently applied to conceal faulty merchandise and flawed concepts, it nonetheless can enhance a product when used with integrity—and taste. Decorators do not simply and mindlessly move elements around to achieve an intangible or intuitive goal: rather, they optimize materials at hand to tap into an aesthetic allure that instills a certain kind of pleasure.

Loos and like-minded late-nineteenth and early-twentieth-century design progressives argued that excessive ornament existed solely to deceive the public into believing they were getting more value for their money—when in fact they were being duped through illusionary conceits. These critics argued that art nouveau (and later art deco or postmodern) decoration on buildings and furniture and in graphic design rarely adds to a product's functionality or durability; it also locks the respective objects in a vault of time that eventually renders everything obsolete. Decoration was therefore the tool of obsolescence.

However, decoration also plays an integral role in the total design scheme. It is not merely wallpaper. (And what's wrong with beautiful wallpaper, anyway?) Good decoration is that which enhances or frames a product or message. The euro paper currency, with its colorful palette and pictorial vibrancy, is much more appealing than the staid US dollar. While the "greenback" is composed of ornate rococo engravings, US bills lack the visual pizzazz of the euro. Of course, visual pizzazz is irrelevant if one is clutching a score of $100 bills; putting the respective face values of the currencies aside, the euro is an indubitably more stimulating object of design because it is a decorative tour de force with a distinct function. One should never underestimate the power of decoration to stimulate the users of design.

Decoration is a marriage of forms (color, line, pattern, letter, picture) that does not overtly tell a story or convey a literal message, but serves to stimulate the senses. Paisley, herringbone, or tartan patterns are decorative, yet nonetheless elicit certain visceral responses. Ziggurat or sunburst designs on the façade of a building or the cover of a brochure spark a chord even when type is absent. Decorative and ornamental design elements are backdrops, yet possess the power to draw attention, which ultimately prepares the audience to receive the message.

It takes as much sophistication to be a decorator as it does to be a wire-framer. A designer who decorates yet does not know how to effectively control, modulate, or create ornamental elements is doomed to produce turgid work. The worst decorative excesses are not the obsessively baroque borders and patterns that are born of an eclectic vision (like the vines and tendrils that strangulated the typical art nouveau poster or page), but the ignorant application of dysfunctional doodads that are total anachronisms. A splendidly ornamented package, including the current crop of boutique teas, soaps, and food wrappers, may cost a little more to produce but still have quantifiable impact on the consumers with discerning tastes who buy them (and who sometimes keep the boxes after the product is used).

There are many different kinds and degrees of decoration and ornamentation. While none of it is really sinful, much of it is trivial. And yet to be a practitioner of this kind of design does not a priori relegate one to inferior status branded with a scarlet (shadowed, inline, and bifurcated) letter "D."

Some designers are great because they are exemplary decorators.

Originally published on *Design Observer*, November 24, 2007.

# DISCUSSION POINTS

- Do you like to decorate?
- Why would ornament be a sin?
- How do you define good ornament or bad ornament?
- Can ornament be meaningful content?

# HARSH
# WORDS
# REDUX

I often refer to this essay by the famed neoclassical graphic designer and illustrator Thomas Maitlin Cleland as the final reading assignment. It speaks well to the disparities between personal opinion and professional criticism. This piece, which was published in 1940 in a smartly designed small booklet, is of its time, to be sure, but also establishes a tone that applies to the present.

Design criticism may be comparatively new, but critical designers are not. During the late nineteenth century, William Morris was known to scold his fellows over the erosion of design standards brought about by the industrial revolution. Two decades later, William Addison Dwiggins routinely complained about the continuous decline in aesthetic virtuosity. The grousing—I mean, reflective critical debate—continued through the twentieth century. One of the not-so-genteel of the designer critiques was "An address delivered at a meeting of the American Institute of Graphic Arts in New York City" on February 5, 1940, "on the occasion of the opening of the Seventeenth Annual exhibition of the Fifty Books of the Year" by Thomas Maitland (T. M.) Cleland (and later published by the AIGA as a keepsake). Cleland's ominously titled "Harsh Words" began thus:

> The generosity of your invitation to me to speak on this important occasion leaves me a trifle bewildered. I am so accustomed to being told to keep my opinions to myself that being thus unexpectedly encouraged to express them gives me some cause to wonder if I have, or ever had, any opinions upon the graphic arts worth expressing.

Whether they were worth expressing was ultimately in the ear of the receiver; nonetheless, Cleland had a lot to say. Thirty-nine pages, over five thousand words' worth of displeasure with the state of the book and typography, and a lot more that he disingenuously hoped "will not be thought an abuse of this kindly tendered privilege."

The AIGA elders doubtless knew what they were in for. This was a celebration of printing and typography, but Cleland, a book designer who designed the first cover of *Fortune Magazine* in 1933, had his sights on bigger game than the 50 Best Books. His mission, he declared, was "to deplore the fifty thousand worst books, which may be seen elsewhere."

"If I can only develop it in terms of a tree," he said of his aesthetic vision, "the tree I have in mind is cultural civilization: one of its limbs is art, and a branch of this we call the graphic arts; and a twig on this branch is printing and typography." Among his prime bugaboos is "the idea that originality is essential to the successful practice of the graphic arts, [and] is more prevalent today than it ever was in the days when the graphic arts were practiced at their best." Responding to the end of the so-called avant-garde era of experimentation, Cleland cautioned, "The current belief that everyone must now be an inventor is too often interpreted to mean that no one need any longer be a workman."

Sound familiar? Today's notion that the computer will undo all the genius the hand hath wrought? "The conscious cultivator of his own individuality will go to extravagant lengths to escape the pains imposed by a standard," Cleland added. Can you hear the cheers, such as the kind punctuating the State of the Union address, following key passages?

Another of Cleland's *bêtes noires* was "the superabsurdity" of modernism. "Embraced with fanatic enthusiasm by many architects and designers is the current quackery called 'Functionalism,'" he wrote. Cleland reveled in ornamentation, so it's to be expected that he argued against "a new gospel for the regeneration of our aesthetic world . . . [that restricted] all design to the function of its object or materials." Like many designers of his day who distrusted the motives and outcomes of a younger generation (e.g., Paul Rand, Lester Beall, Bradbury Thompson), Cleland saw modernism as merely the latest among "the new religions and philosophies that have paraded in and out of our social history for countless generations."

While attacking the coupling of ideology with design ("the simple addition of an 'ism,'" he sneered), Cleland aimed even more barbs at the popular Streamline style, as practiced by the industrial designers Raymond Loewy, Norman Bel Geddes, Henry Dreyfuss, and Walter Dorwin Teague). This work he decried as "unsightly" and a reflection of "mass vulgarity."

Cleland reached his critical crescendo when discoursing on type and printing. He accused the modernists of simplifying traditional forms of type "as you might simplify a man by cutting his hands and feet off." He added, "You can no more dispense with the essential features of the written or printed Roman alphabet, ladies and gentlemen, than you can dispense with the accents and intonations of human speech. This is simplification for simpletons, and these are block letters for blockheads."

"We hear now of 'left wing' artists," he said about designers with noncommercial, save-the-world ambitions. "As nearly as I can discover, these are to be recognized by their contempt for any sort of craftsmanship and peculiar ability to keep their drawings clean. They make penury a pious virtue, and they are not infrequently big with pretension to being the only serious interpreters of life and truth." Even back then, eh? But Cleland reserved bile for the slick professional too, "the school of 'economic royalists' who have made of art a commercial opportunity." That is to say, industrial designers with large staffs, who have "welded art and commerce so successfully that it is nearly impossible to tell them apart."

What Cleland was looking for was "somewhere between the two," an artist not quite poor enough to be picturesque, just well enough off "to keep his collar and his drawings clean."

My point in quoting Cleland's "Harsh Words" is not to ridicule him for being reactionary or curmudgeonly. He was a highly respected designer who had the courage to stand before a (substantially unsympathetic) audience and debate issues important at the time. He didn't have the comfort of ducking behind a blogger's pseudonym, which accounts for the humility that took some of the sting out of his rant. "I humbly pray, ladies and gentlemen," he wrote, "that you will apply no instruments of precision to my words—they are the best I could find in this emergency for saying what I believe to be true. If you think me guilty of exaggeration, the foregoing remarks are my only defense. But if you accuse me of being facetious, I will tell you that I have never been more serious in my life."

Originally published as "Harsh Words from T. M. Cleland" on *Design Observer*, December 14, 2009.

# Acknowledgments

As always, much gratitude to Tad Crawford, publisher, for his continued faith in and encouragement for my books on design, thirty-five of which have been published by Allworth Press. To David Rhodes, president of SVA NYC, for his continued support and leadership. Without these people none of this is possible.

With sincere appreciation to Chamois Holschuh for her editorial stewardship, as always an invaluable part of the process. I can never say enough in tribute about the terrific job that designer and collaborator Rick Landers brings to my projects, so I'll just say thanks!

Most of these essays were originally published in other venues—the primary outlets have been *Print* magazine and Imprint.com. Thanks to Zachary Petit for his editorial skills and consultations. I've written regularly for DesignObserver.com as well. Thanks to Betsy Vardell for her acute editorial direction and Jessica Helfand for her support. A few have appeared in my former T-Style "Graphic Content" column at NYTimes.com and on Atlantic.com, and a couple are reprised from books and catalogs I've had the pleasure to work on.

A few of the essays were done for *EYE* magazine, at different periods under Rick Poynor and John Walters. Hard taskmasters both, I appreciate their respective points of view.

A number of colleagues have made it possible to have the time, energy, and resources for my writing projects—many tips of the hat to Lita Talarico, Mirko Ilic, Jeff Roth, Beth Kleber, Debbie Millman, and my best of all friends, Seymour Chwast.

I am particularly indebted to a leader of the "graphic design history movement": Victor Margolin, who passed away as I was completing this book. I always looked over my shoulder to see whether or not, given his invaluable counsel, he approved of my musings.

Finally, I'd be nowhere without the embrace of my incredibly talented and inspiring family, my wife Louise Fili and son Nicolas Heller (New York Nico).

—Steven Heller, December 2019

# Index

# Index

# Index

# Index

# Index

# Index

**About Design** by Gordon Salchow with Foreword by Michael Bierut and Afterword by Katherine McCoy ($6^1/_8 \times 6^1/_8$, 208 pages, paperback, $19.99)

**Becoming a Design Entrepreneur** by Steven Heller and Lita Talarico (6 × 9, 208 pages, paperback, $19.99)

**Brand Thinking and Other Noble Pursuits** by Debbie Millman with Rob Walker (6 × 9, 336 pages, paperback, $19.95)

**Citizen Designer (Second Edition)** by Steven Heller and Véronique Vienne (6 × 9, 312 pages, paperback, $22.99)

**Design Literacy** by Steven Heller with Rick Poynor (6 × 9, 304 pages, paperback, $22.50)

**Design Thinking** by Thomas Lockwood (6 × 9, 304 pages, paperback, $24.95)

**Designers Don't Read** by Austin Howe with Fredrik Averin ($5^1/_2 \times 8^1/_2$, 224 pages, paperback, $19.95)

**The Education of a Graphic Designer** by Steven Heller (6 × 9, 380 pages, paperback, $19.99)

**The Elements of Graphic Design** by Alex W. White (8 × 10, 224 pages, paperback, $29.95)

**Graphic Design History** Edited by Steven Heller and Georgette Balance ($6^1/_2 \times 10$, 352 pages, paperback, $29.99)

**Graphic Design Rants and Raves** by Steven Heller (7 × 9, 200 pages, paperback, $19.99)

**How to Think Like a Great Graphic Designer** by Debbie Millman (6 × 9, 248 pages, paperback, $24.95)

**Listening to Type** by Alex W. White (8 × 10, 272 pages, paperback, $29.99)

**Looking Closer 5** Edited by Michael Bierut, William Drenttel, and Steven Heller ($6^1/_2 \times 8^7/_8$, 256 pages, paperback, $21.95)

**POP** by Steven Heller (6 × 9, 288 pages, paperback, $24.95)

**Teaching Design** by Meredith Davis (6 × 9, 216 pages, paperback, $24.99)

**Teaching Graphic Design (Second Edition)** by Steven Heller (6 × 9, 312 pages, paperback, $24.99)

**Vintage Graphic Design** by Steven Heller and Louis Fili (8 × 10, 208 pages, paperback, $19.99)

*To see our complete catalog or to order online, please visit www.allworth.com.*